War in the Persian Gulf Almanac

From Operation Desert Storm to Operation Iraqi Freedom

War in the Persian Gulf Almanac

From Operation Desert Storm to Operation Iraqi Freedom

LAURIE COLLIER HILLSTROM

Julie Carnagie,
Project Editor

U•X•L
An imprint of Thomson Gale,
a part of The Thomson Corporation

Detroit • New York • San Francisco • San Diego • New Haven, Conn. • Waterville, Maine • London • Munich

THOMSON

GALE

War in the Persian Gulf Almanac: From Operation Desert Storm to Operation Iraqi Freedom

Laurie Collier Hillstrom

Project Editor
Julie L. Carnagie

Permissions
Shalice Shah-Caldwell

Imaging and Multimedia
Lezlie Light, Mike Logusz, Christine O'Bryan, Kelly A. Quin

Product Design
Pamela Galbreath

Composition
Evi Seoud

Manufacturing
Rita Wimberley

Library of Congress Control Number: 2004005309

Printed in the United States of America
10 9 8 7 6 5 4 3 2 1

ISBN 0-7876-6563-0

This title is also available as an e-book. ISBN 0-7876-9347-2
Contact your Gale sales representative for ordering information.

Contents

Reader's Guide

War in the Persian Gulf Almanac: From Operation Desert Storm to Operation Iraqi Freedom presents a comprehensive overview of the U.S.-led wars against Iraq that took place in 1991 and 2003. The volume's twelve chapters are arranged chronologically and cover all aspects of the conflict. *War in the Persian Gulf Almanac: From Operation Desert Storm to Operation Iraqi Freedom* begins by describing the history of the Middle East and Saddam Hussein's rise to power in Iraq. It then details Iraq's 1990 invasion of Kuwait and the international response, culminating in Operation Desert Storm in 1991. The volume continues by describing the decade of economic sanctions and weapons inspections in the aftermath of the 1991 Persian Gulf War, and the shift in U.S. policy toward "regime change" in Iraq. It concludes by describing the battles of Operation Iraqi Freedom, the fall of Baghdad to U.S. forces in April 2003, and the challenges of building a peaceful, democratic Iraq.

Features

War in the Persian Gulf Almanac: From Operation Desert Storm to Operation Iraqi Freedom includes informative sidebars, some containing brief biographies of people associated with the conflicts in Iraq, others focusing on interesting facts about pivotal issues and events. Approximately sixty black-and-white photographs and maps enliven the work. *War in the Persian Gulf Almanac: From Operation Desert Storm to Operation Iraqi Freedom* also includes a timeline of important events, "Words to Know" and "People to Know" sections, and a list of research and activity ideas with suggestions for study questions, group projects, and oral and dramatic presentations. *War in the Persian Gulf Almanac: From Operation Desert Storm to Operation Iraqi Freedom* concludes with a bibliography of sources for further reading and a subject index.

War in the Persian Gulf Reference Library: From Operation Desert Storm to Operation Iraqi Freedom

War in the Persian Gulf Almanac: From Operation Desert Storm to Operation Iraqi Freedom is only one component of a three-volume War in the Persian Gulf: From Operation Desert Storm to Operation Iraqi Freedom Reference Library. The other two titles in this multivolume set are:

- *War in the Persian Gulf Biographies: From Operation Desert Storm to Operation Iraqi Freedom* presents profiles of thirty men and women who participated in or were affected by the 1991 Persian Gulf War and the 2003 Iraq War. The volume covers such key people as political leaders George H. W. Bush, George W. Bush, Saddam Hussein, Yassir Arafat, Tony Blair, and Jacques Chirac; military leaders Colin Powell and H. Norman Schwarzkopf; journalists Christiane Amanpour, Peter Arnett, and Bob Simon; and prisoners of war Jeffrey Zaun and Jessica Lynch. The volume is filled with photographs, sidebars, a timeline of key events, a glossary, a "People to Know" section, sources for further reading, and an index.

- *War in the Persian Gulf Primary Sources: From Operation Desert Storm to Operation Iraqi Freedom* presents twelve full or excerpted documents related to the 1991 and 2003 U.S.-led wars against Iraq. These documents range from notable speeches that mark important points in the conflicts to personal diaries and letters that reflect the experiences of ordinary soldiers and civilians. The excerpts are arranged chronologically, beginning with Iraqi leader Saddam Hussein's decision to invade Kuwait in 1990 and ending with an Iraqi citizen's 2003 Internet diary describing conditions in Baghdad under U.S. occupation. Each excerpt has a glossary that runs alongside the reprinted document to identify unfamiliar terms and ideas contained within the material. The volume also includes photographs, sidebars, a timeline of key events, a glossary, a "People to Know" section, sources for further reading, and an index.

- A cumulative index of all three titles in War in the Persian Gulf Reference Library: From Operation Desert Storm to Operation Iraqi Freedom is also available.

Advisors

A note of appreciation is extended to the *War in the Persian Gulf Almanac: From Operation Desert Storm to Operation Iraqi Freedom* advisors who provided invaluable suggestions when the work was in its formative stages:

Erik D. France
Librarian
University of Liggett Upper School
Grosse Pointe Woods, Michigan

Ann West LaPrise
Junior High/Elementary Librarian
Huron School District
New Boston, Michigan

Angela Leeper
Educational Consultant
Wake Forest, North Carolina

Comments and Suggestions

We welcome your comments on *War in the Persian Gulf Almanac: From Operation Desert Storm to Operation Iraqi Freedom* and suggestions for other topics in history to consider. Please write: Editors, *War in the Persian Gulf Almanac: From Operation Desert Storm to Operation Iraqi Freedom*, U•X•L, 27500 Drake Road, Farmington Hills, MI 48331-3535; call toll-free 800-877-4253; fax to 248-699-8097; or send e-mail via http://www.gale.com.

Timeline of Events

1922   British High Commissioner Sir Percy Cox establishes the borders of Iraq and Kuwait.

1927   British explorers make the largest oil strike in the world to date at Kirkuk in northern Iraq.

1932   Iraq gains its independence from British colonial rule.

1937   Saddam Hussein is born in a village near Tikrit, Iraq.

1961   Kuwait gains its independence from British colonial rule.

1968   The Baath Party takes control of the government of Iraq.

1979   Hussein becomes president of Iraq.

1979   The government of nearby Iran is overthrown by Islamic fundamentalists under the Ayatollah Khomeini.

1980   Iraq declares war against Iran.

1983   Iraq uses chemical weapons for the first time during the Iran-Iraq War.

1988   The Iran-Iraq War ends.

1988 Iraq uses chemical weapons against the Kurdish people of northern Iraq.

January, 1989 George H. W. Bush is inaugurated thirty-ninth president of the United States.

July 17, 1990 Hussein threatens to use force against Kuwait.

July 24, 1990 Tens of thousands of Iraqi troops begin gathering along the Kuwaiti border.

July 25, 1990 Hussein meets with April Glaspie, the U.S. ambassador to Iraq.

July 31, 1990 Iraqi and Kuwaiti officials meet in Jedda, Saudi Arabia, to discuss Iraq's concerns about border issues and oil prices.

August 2, 1990 Iraq invades Kuwait.

August 2, 1990 The United Nations (UN) Security Council passes Resolution 660, condemning Iraq's invasion of Kuwait.

August 6, 1990 The UN Security Council passes Resolution 661, imposing economic sanctions on Iraq.

August 6, 1990 Saudi Arabia agrees to allow American and other foreign troops into the country.

August 7, 1990 U.S. President George H. W. Bush begins sending American troops to Saudi Arabia for Operation Desert Shield.

August 8, 1990 Hussein announces the annexation of Kuwait by Iraq.

August 10, 1990 The UN Security Council passes Resolution 662, condemning Iraq's annexation of Kuwait.

August 15, 1990 Hussein makes peace with Iran by agreeing to all conditions of the 1988 cease-fire that ended the Iran-Iraq War.

August 18, 1990 Iraq announces that it plans to hold Westerners who had been in Iraq and Kuwait at the time of the invasion and use them as "human shields" at military targets.

September 1, 1990 Iraq begins releasing some Western women and children it had been holding hostage since the invasion.

September 9, 1990 U.S. President George H. W. Bush meets with Soviet President Mikhail Gorbachev at the Helsinki Summit; the two leaders reach agreement on a plan to deal with Iraq.

November 1, 1990 More than one million refugees have fled from Iraq and Kuwait since the invasion.

November 8, 1990 Bush announces the deployment of an additional two hundred thousand American troops to the Persian Gulf.

November 29, 1990 The UN Security Council passes Resolution 678, which establishes a deadline of January 15, 1991, for Iraq to withdraw from Kuwait and authorizes members to use force if Iraq fails to comply.

December 6, 1990 Iraq releases remaining Western hostages.

January 9, 1991 U.S. Secretary of State James Baker meets with Iraqi Foreign Minister Tariq Aziz in Geneva, Switzerland, but they fail to reach an agreement to avoid war.

January 12, 1991 The U.S. Congress authorizes the president to use force to liberate Kuwait.

January 15, 1991 Iraqi forces fail to withdraw from Kuwait by UN deadline.

January 16, 1991 President Bush makes a televised speech announcing the start of the Persian Gulf War.

January 17, 1991 A U.S.-led coalition launches an air war against Iraq to begin Operation Desert Storm.

January 18, 1991 Iraq begins firing Scud missiles at Israel.

January 20, 1991 U.S. patriot missiles successfully intercept Iraqi Scud missiles aimed at Dharan, Saudi Arabia.

January 22, 1991 Iraqi soldiers begin setting fire to Kuwait's oil production facilities.

January 23, 1991 U.S. Army General Colin Powell announces that the coalition has achieved air superiority.

January 25, 1991 Iraqi forces release millions of gallons of oil into the Persian Gulf.

January 30, 1991 Iraqi forces capture the Saudi Arabian border town of Khafji.

January 31, 1991 Saudi Arabian troops backed by U.S. Marines reclaim Khafji after an intense battle.

February 13, 1991 U.S. laser-guided bombs destroy a bunker in Baghdad, killing more than one hundred Iraqi civilians.

February 15, 1991 Iraq offers to withdraw from Kuwait but coalition leaders find Iraq's conditions unacceptable and reject the offer.

February 18, 1991 Soviet President Gorbachev announces a new plan to end the war, but Bush rejects it because it does not meet all of the UN Security Council resolutions.

February 22, 1991 Bush sets a deadline of the following day for Iraqi troops to withdraw from Kuwait or face a ground war.

February 24, 1991 The U.S.-led coalition launches a ground war against Iraq.

February 26, 1991 An Iraqi Scud missile hits a U.S. Army camp in Dharan, Saudi Arabia, killing twenty-eight American soldiers.

February 27, 1991 Kuwait City is liberated by coalition forces.

February 28, 1991 Bush declares victory over Iraq and orders a cease-fire.

March 2, 1991 Shiite Muslims in southern Iraq and Kurds in northern Iraq stage rebellions against Hussein's rule; Hussein violently crushes the attempts to overthrow his government.

March 3, 1991 Iraq agrees to all allied terms for a permanent cease-fire.

April 3, 1991 The United Nations passes Resolution 687, formally ending the Persian Gulf War.

April 15, 1991 The United Nations conducts the first international weapons inspections in Iraq.

November 1991 The last oil-well fires are extinguished in Kuwait.

1992 The United States establishes a "no-fly zone" in southern Iraq to protect the country's Shiite minority from an attack by the Iraqi air force.

January 1993 Bill Clinton is inaugurated the fortieth president of the United States.

1993 Iraq refuses to cooperate with UN weapons inspectors, and the United States responds by firing cruise missiles at a suspected chemical weapons plant near Baghdad.

1993 Iraqi operatives attempt to assassinate former U.S. President Bush during his visit to Kuwait; the United States retaliates by destroying Iraqi intelligence headquarters with cruise missiles.

1994 Iraq moves troops toward the Kuwait border, but pulls back when the United States sends aircraft carriers to the Persian Gulf.

1995 The UN Security Council passes Resolution 986, which allows Iraq to sell limited amounts of oil in international markets and use the proceeds to buy food.

1995 The Iraqi National Congress launches an unsuccessful coup against Hussein.

1996 Iraqi troops capture Erbil, the capital of the Kurdish-controlled region of northern Iraq. The United States responds by expanding the "no-fly zone" to northern Iraq.

1997 The U.S. House of Representatives launches an investigation into the possible causes of the mysterious collection of ailments among Gulf War veterans known as Gulf War syndrome.

1998 Iraq stops cooperating with UN weapons inspectors, and inspectors leave Iraq.

1998 U.S. and British forces launch Operation Desert Fox, a bombing campaign aimed at destroying suspected weapons of mass destruction in Iraq.

January 2001 George W. Bush is inaugurated the forty-first president of the United States.

September 11, 2001 The terrorist group Al Qaeda hijacks four commercial airliners and crashes two into the

World Trade Center in New York City, one into the Pentagon near Washington, D.C., and a fourth thwarted attempt into an empty Pennsylvania field, killing more than three thousand people.

January 29, 2002 U.S. President George W. Bush makes his "axis of evil" speech, officially expanding the fight against terrorism to include nations that shelter terrorists or provide weapons, training, or financial support for their activities. Among the countries that he accuses of supporting terrorists are Iraq, Iran, and North Korea.

September 12, 2002 Bush challenges the United Nations to enforce its resolutions against Iraq that ended the 1991 Persian Gulf War.

September 16, 2002 Iraq says it will allow UN inspections to resume "without conditions."

October 11, 2002 The U.S. Congress authorizes the use of military force against Iraq.

November 8, 2002 The UN Security Council passes Resolution 1441, which authorizes a new round of weapons inspections in Iraq and promises "serious consequences" if Hussein fails to comply.

November 18, 2002 Iraq allows UN weapons inspectors to return to the country after a four-year absence.

January 28, 2003 In his second State of the Union address, Bush cites British intelligence reports claiming that Iraq tried to acquire uranium from Africa to build nuclear weapons.

February 5, 2003 U.S. Secretary of State Colin Powell presents evidence of Iraqi weapons programs to the United Nations.

February 14, 2003 Head UN weapons inspector Hans Blix challenges Powell's evidence and praises Iraq's cooperation with inspections.

February 15, 2003 Large-scale antiwar protests take place in dozens of cities around the world.

February 24, 2003 The United States introduces a new UN resolution authorizing the use of military force to disarm Iraq, but France threatens to veto the resolution.

March 17, 2003 Bush withdraws the proposed UN resolution and gives Hussein and his two sons forty-eight hours to leave Iraq or face a U.S.-led invasion.

March 19, 2003 The United States launches air strikes against targets in Iraq to begin the 2003 Iraq War.

March 20, 2003 U.S. and British ground forces begin advancing into Iraq.

March 21, 2003 Coalition forces launch the "shock and awe" bombing campaign.

March 23, 2003 Members of the U.S. Army's 507th Maintenance Company are ambushed in the city of Nasiriyah.

April 4, 2003 U.S. forces capture Saddam International Airport outside Baghdad.

April 5, 2003 U.S. tanks roll through the streets of Baghdad for the first time.

April 7, 2003 British forces take control of the city of Basra in southern Iraq.

April 9, 2003 A statue of Hussein is toppled in central Baghdad's Firdos Square, symbolizing the fall of the Iraqi regime; looting and violence erupts in the city.

April 14, 2003 The Pentagon declares that major combat operations in Iraq have ended.

April 15, 2003 The first meeting to plan Iraq's future is held in the ancient city of Ur.

May 1, 2003 Bush makes his historic speech aboard the aircraft carrier USS *Abraham Lincoln,* announcing that major combat operations in Iraq are over and that the Iraqi people have been freed from Hussein's rule.

May 12, 2003 American diplomat L. Paul Bremer III arrives in Baghdad to head the Coalition Provisional Authority, the U.S.-led civil administration in charge of Iraq's reconstruction.

May 22, 2003 The UN Security Council passes Resolution 1483, formally recognizing the United States and Great Britain as "occupying powers" in Iraq.

July 6, 2003 Former U.S. Ambassador Joseph Wilson accuses the Bush administration of exaggerating the threat posed by Iraq's alleged weapons programs.

July 13, 2003 The Iraq Governing Council is formed as the first interim government of the new Iraq; it consists of twenty-five prominent Iraqis from diverse ethnic and religious backgrounds.

July 22, 2003 Hussein's two sons, Uday and Qusay, are killed in a firefight with U.S. troops in Mosul.

August 7, 2003 A car bomb explodes outside the Jordanian embassy in Baghdad, marking the first terrorist attack following the fall of Saddam Hussein.

August 19, 2003 A truck bomb explodes outside the UN headquarters in Baghdad, killing twenty-three people, including Sergio Vieira de Mello, the UN Special Representative to Iraq.

August 31, 2003 The number of U.S. troops killed in Iraq following the end of major combat operations surpasses the number killed during the war.

September 7, 2003 Bush asks the U.S. Congress to approve his request for $87 billion to pay for ongoing military and rebuilding efforts in Afghanistan and Iraq.

November 27, 2003 On Thanksgiving, Bush makes a surprise visit to U.S. military forces in Baghdad.

December 13, 2003 Former Iraqi leader Saddam Hussein is captured by U.S. forces.

Words to Know

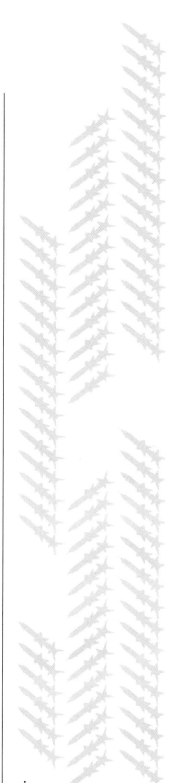

A

Al Qaeda: A radical Islamic terrorist group responsible for the September 11, 2001, terrorist attacks against the United States.

Annex: To incorporate a country or territory into another country.

Arab League: An alliance of twenty Arab nations and the Palestine Liberation Organization that promotes political, military, and economic cooperation in the Arab world.

Arabs: People of North Africa and the Middle East who speak the Arabic language.

B

Baath Party: A radical political movement founded in the 1940s with the goal of uniting the Arab world and creating one powerful Arab state.

C

Civilians: People not involved in fighting a war, including women and children.

Coalition: A temporary alliance of countries working toward a common goal.

Coalition Provisional Authority: The U.S.-run civil agency in charge of Iraq's 2003 postwar reconstruction.

Cold War: A period of political tension and military rivalry between the United States and the Soviet Union that began in the 1940s and ended with the collapse of the Soviet Union in 1989.

E

Economic sanctions: Trade restrictions intended to punish a country for breaking international law.

F

Fedayeen: A group of Iraqi paramilitary fighters that was intensely loyal to Iraqi President Saddam Hussein.

G

Geneva Conventions: A set of rules developed in Geneva, Swizterland, between 1864 and 1949 that are intended to guarantee the human treatment of enemy soldiers and prisoners and the protection of civilians during wartime.

I

Insurgency: Organized resistance against an established government or occupying force.

Iran: A non-Arab nation in the Middle East that came under control of Shiite Muslim fundamentalists in 1979 and fought against Iraq during the Iran-Iraq War (1980–88).

Iraq Governing Council (IGC): The first transitional government in Iraq following the 2003 fall of Iraqi President Saddam Hussein; its membership included twenty-five prominent Iraqis whose political, ethnic, and religious backgrounds reflected the diversity of Iraq's population.

Israel: A Middle Eastern state created by the United Nations in 1948 as a homeland for all Jewish people. It is now the scene of major conflicts between the Israeli people and the Palestinians.

K

Kurds: A group of non-Arab Muslim people of northern Iraq who opposed Iraqi President Saddam Hussein's government.

M

Muslims: People who practice the religion of Islam.

O

Organization of Oil Exporting Countries (OPEC): An organization formed in the 1960s by the world's major oil-producing nations to coordinate policies and ensure stable oil prices in world markets.

Ottomans: A group of non-Arab Turkish invaders who conquered much of the Middle East around 1500 and ruled over a vast empire until 1920.

P

Palestine Liberation Organization (PLO): A political organization representing displaced Palestinians. The main goals of the PLO include reclaiming lost territory from Israel and establishing an independent Palestinian state.

Palestinians: An Arab people whose ancestors lived in the region that is now covered by the Jewish state of Israel. The creation of Israel in 1948 displaced hundreds of thousands of Palestinians and contributed to later conflicts in the Middle East.

R

Reconstruction: The process of rebuilding a country's infrastructure, government, and economy following a war.

Republican Guard: An elite, 100,000-man force that was the best-trained and best-equipped part of Iraq's army.

S

Shiite: A branch of the Islamic religion practiced by 15 percent of the world's Muslims, but 60 percent of Iraq's population.

Sunni: A branch of the Islamic religion practiced by 85 percent of the world's Muslims, but only 20 percent of Iraq's population.

T

Taliban: A radical Islamic group that took over the government of Afghanistan in 1996. The Taliban sheltered Osama bin Laden and Al Qaeda, the terrorists behind the attacks against the United States on September 11, 2001.

U

United Nations Security Council: The division of the United Nations charged with maintaining international peace and security. It consists of five permanent member nations (the United States, Russia, Great Britain, France, and China) and ten elected members that serve two-year terms.

People to Know

A

Madeleine Albright (1937–): U.S. ambassador to the United Nations (1993–97) and U.S. secretary of state (1997–2000) under President Bill Clinton.

Tariq Aziz (1936–): Iraqi foreign minister and lead negotiator during the 1991 Persian Gulf War who was captured by coalition forces during the 2003 Iraq War.

B

James Baker (1930–): U.S. secretary of state during the 1991 Persian Gulf War.

Ahmed Hassan al-Bakr (1914–1982): Older cousin of Saddam Hussein and Baath Party leader who served as the president of Iraq from 1968 to 1979.

Osama bin Laden (1957–): Saudi-born Muslim cleric who formed the Al Qaeda terrorist group and organized the September 11, 2001, attacks against the United States.

Tony Blair (1953–): Prime Minister of Great Britain during the 2003 Iraq War.

L. Paul Bremer III (1941–): American diplomat and head of the Coalition Provisional Authority, the group charged with Iraq's reconstruction following the 2003 war.

George H. W. Bush (1924–): President of the United States (1989–93) during the 1991 Persian Gulf War.

George W. Bush (1946–): President of the United States (2001–) during the 2003 Iraq War; son of former president, George H. W. Bush.

C

Dick Cheney (1941–) Served as U.S. secretary of defense during the 1991 Persian Gulf War and vice president during the 2003 Iraq War.

Jacques Chirac (1932–) President of France who led international opposition to the 2003 Iraq War.

Bill Clinton (1946–) President of the United States from 1993 to 2001.

Sir Percy Cox (1864–1937): British government official who established the modern borders of Iraq, Saudi Arabia, and Kuwait in 1921.

H

Saddam Hussein (1937–): President of Iraq (1979–2003) during the 1991 Persian Gulf War who was removed from power during the 2003 Iraq War.

K

Ayatollah Khomeini (1900–1989): Islamic religious leader and outspoken opponent of Saddam Hussein who ruled Iran during the Iran-Iraq War (1980–88).

M

Ali Hassan al-Majid (1941–): Iraqi army general known as "Chemical Ali" for allegedly ordering the use of chemical weapons against the Kurdish people of northern Iraq. He was captured following the 2003 Iraq War.

P

Colin Powell (1937–): U.S. military general and chairman of the Joint Chiefs of Staff during the 1991 Persian Gulf War; also served as secretary of state during the 2003 Iraq War.

Q

Abdul Karim Qassem (1914–1963): Military ruler of Iraq from 1958 to 1963, when he was assassinated by members of the Baath Party.

R

Donald Rumsfeld (1932–): U.S. secretary of defense who played a leading role in deciding military strategy for the 2003 Iraq War.

S

Jaber al-Ahmed al-Sabah (1926–): Emir (ruler) of Kuwait during the 1991 Persian Gulf War.

Mohammed Said al-Sahhaf (1940–): Iraqi information minister during the 2003 Iraq War. He became known as "Baghdad Bob" and "Comical Ali" due to his defiant and overly optimistic statements to the media.

H. Norman Schwarzkopf (1934–): U.S. Army general and commander of allied forces during Operation Desert Storm.

T

Margaret Thatcher (1925–): Prime Minister of Great Britain during the 1990 Iraqi invasion of Kuwait.

Research and Activity Ideas

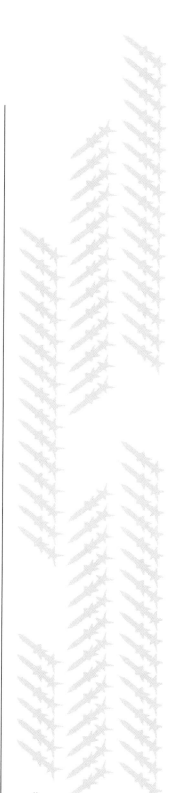

The following research and activity ideas are intended to offer suggestions for complementing social studies and history curricula; to trigger additional ideas for enhancing learning; and to provide cross-disciplinary projects for library and classroom use.

Many of the causes of tension between Iraq and Kuwait in the 1980s can be traced back to the era of European rule over the Middle East. Make a list of all of the reasons Iraqi leaders gave for invading Kuwait in August 1990. Make check marks next to the ones that stem from the decisions made decades earlier by British colonial rulers. What other sources of political tension and turmoil in the Middle East might be attributed to the period of European rule?

Read a biography of Iraqi leader Saddam Hussein. What factors in his early life, and in the history of Iraq, may have led him to become a brutal dictator who used violence to eliminate his political opponents? Write a one-page essay supporting your answer.

Some historians claim that the 1991 Persian Gulf War could have been avoided through clear and open communication between Iraqi and Western leaders. Instead, the dialogue between the two sides was filled with mixed messages and misunderstandings in the months leading up to the war. Create a chart as a class. One side will list Iraqi statements and actions that were misunderstood by Western leaders, and the other will show Western statements and actions that were misinterpreted by Saddam Hussein. Refer to the charts while discussing how Saddam Hussein came to believe that Western nations would not get involved if Iraq invaded Kuwait.

Divide the class into three groups. One group will play the role of Iraqi negotiators, another will play the role of Kuwaiti negotiators, and the third group will play the role of representatives of other Arab nations in the Persian Gulf region. Pretend that it is August 1, 1990, and conduct mock negotiations aimed at avoiding Iraq's invasion of Kuwait.

The United States supported Iraq during its eight-year war against Iran (1980–88). Two years later, the United States formed a military coalition to fight against Iraq in the Persian Gulf War. Imagine that you are a high-ranking official in George H. W. Bush's administration. Write an editorial for the *Washington Post* that explains the changes in U.S. policy toward Iraq.

Iraq's 1990 invasion of Kuwait created a split in the Arab world. Many Arab nations condemned the invasion and sent troops to Saudi Arabia as part of the U.S.-led coalition against Iraq. Yet several other Arab nations expressed their support for Iraq. Why did the leaders of Jordan and the Palestine Liberation Organization (PLO) choose to support Iraq? What did Saddam Hussein do in order to gain the support of some of his Arab neighbors? Pretend that you are the leader of an Arab nation, like King Hussein of Jordan; Yasir Arafat of the PLO; or King Fahd of Saudi Arabia, and explain your decision to support or oppose Iraq in an oral presentation.

Many Americans opposed President George H. W. Bush's decision to send U.S. troops to the Persian Gulf in 1991 to force Iraq to withdraw from Kuwait. Some antiwar activists felt that the United States was only interested in defending Kuwait because it possessed huge underground oil reserves. What role did the U.S. dependence on foreign oil play in Bush's decision to fight the Persian Gulf War? Can you find other examples from history in which one country invaded another but the United States reacted differently?

Iraq committed a multitude of human rights abuses during its occupation of Kuwait and the 1991 Persian Gulf War. For example, Iraqi troops arrested and tortured Kuwaiti citizens, destroyed Kuwaiti property and oil facilities, used foreign citizens as "human shields" to defend potential military targets against coalition air strikes, and mistreated coalition prisoners of war in violation of the Geneva Conventions. Pretend that you are Iraqi Foreign Minister Tariq Aziz. How do you justify or defend such actions?

Create a map of the coalition ground war strategy during Operation Desert Storm. Show the class how coalition leaders succeeded in deceiving the Iraqi forces. Explain the role of the air war in ensuring the strategy's effectiveness.

Before the ground war began on February 24, 1991, many military experts warned that the coalition should prepare for months of intensive battles against the hardened Iraqi troops in their dug-in defensive positions. These experts also predicted that the coalition forces could suffer thousands of casualties. As it turned out, the ground war lasted only 100 hours and cost the lives of 240 coalition soldiers. Think about the factors that favored each side before the war began. Write a one-page essay explaining why you think the coalition victory was so decisive.

The 1991 coalition ground assault rolled over Iraqi defenses, forcing thousands of Iraqi soldiers to surrender and thousands of others to make a hasty retreat. Considering the weakened condition of the Iraqi military, many observers questioned President George H. W. Bush's decision to end the war rather than pushing on toward Baghdad and removing Iraqi President Saddam Hussein from power. Make a list of the reasons that Bush gave for ending the war when he did. What changed over the next dozen years to convince President George W. Bush to launch another war against Iraq in 2003 to remove Hussein from power?

Research the experiences of American soldiers during Operation Desert Shield, Operation Desert Storm, and Operation Iraqi Freedom. Imagine that you are a member of the U.S. forces that took part in one of these military operations. Write a letter to your family back home describing your imaginary experiences.

Choose a newspaper based in a major city near your hometown. Research that newspaper's coverage of the 1991 Persian Gulf War. What was its editorial position on the conflict? Did this position change before, during, or after the war? What is the same paper's editorial position on the 2003 war in Iraq?

Some historians have referred to Iraq as three countries in one. Why would they say this? What effect did the ethnic and religious division of Iraq have on Saddam Hussein's government? What effect will it have on U.S. efforts to establish a democratic government in Iraq?

Upon returning home from the Persian Gulf in 1991, thousands of American soldiers suffered from a collection of mysterious illnesses that eventually became known as Gulf War syndrome. The U.S. government initially denied that the veterans' symptoms were related to their service in the Persian Gulf War and claimed that they were suffering the effects of stress. Why would the government be reluctant to admit that Gulf War syndrome existed? Compare the government's reaction to American veterans' complaints about the effects of exposure to Agent Orange during the Vietnam War (1954–75).

In the dozen years between the 1991 Persian Gulf War and the 2003 Iraq War, the United Nations maintained economic sanctions against Iraq. Many experts claimed that the sanctions had little effect on Saddam Hussein's government while causing tremendous hardships for the Iraqi people and contributing to the deaths of 500,000 Iraqi children. The assistant secretary general of the United Nations, Denis Halliday, resigned in protest over the effect of the sanctions. But U.S. Secretary of State Madeleine Albright defended the policy in a famous "60 Minutes" interview with Lesley Stahl. Assign three students to participate in a mock interview. One student will portray Stahl and conduct the interview, one student will portray Albright and defend the sanctions, and the third student will portray Halliday and oppose the sanctions.

After the 2003 Iraq War removed Saddam Hussein from power, a massive search failed to uncover any evidence of weapons of mass destruction in Iraq. In the years following the 1991 Persian Gulf War, Hussein and other Iraqi leaders consistently claimed that Iraq had ended its weapons programs, yet they also refused to cooperate with UN weapons inspectors. If Hussein had nothing to hide, why did he not cooperate fully with UN demands in the months leading up to the 2003 Iraq War? Do you think his cooperation would have prevented the war? Write a one-page essay exploring these questions.

Following the terrorist attacks of September 11, 2001, the George W. Bush administration developed a sweeping new foreign policy doctrine (statement of fundamental government rules or principles). The Bush doctrine held that the United States had the right to address perceived threats to its security or interests preemptively. In other words, the Bush administration argued that the United States could attack another country in order to prevent a possible future war, rather than only in response to an actual attack against the United States or its allies. The administration used this policy to justify the 2003 invasion of Iraq. Some world leaders expressed strong reservations about the Bush doctrine, questioning the wisdom and legality of the preemptive use of military force. Divide the class into two groups to debate the pros and cons of this new foreign policy.

On February 24, 2003, the United States and Great Britain introduced a new resolution to the United Nations Security Council. The proposed resolution specifically authorized UN member nations to use military force to disarm Iraq. The fifteen nations on the Security Council engaged in weeks of heated debate over the resolution. The United States finally withdrew the proposed resolution and launched a military invasion of Iraq without UN support. Select fifteen students from the class. Assign each student the role of a nation that sat on the UN Security Council in February 2003. Have each student present his or her country's position on the issue, then have the entire class vote on the proposed resolution.

U.S. military strategy differed significantly from the 1991 Persian Gulf War to the 2003 Iraq War. In 1991, for example, the coalition engaged in six weeks of air strikes before launching a ground war. But in 2003, the "shock and awe" bombing campaign started at the same time as the "wave of steel" ground assault. Compare and contrast the U.S. military strategy in the two wars. How did the different goals, assumptions, and available weapons and technology affect the planning for the two conflicts?

During the 2003 Iraq War, the U.S. military issued press credentials to more than 2,500 members of the media. About 600 journalists chose to "embed" themselves in military units and report on the action as it took place. The remaining 2,000 covered the war as "unilateral" journalists, either traveling around Iraq on their own or reporting from Baghdad under the watchful eye of Iraqi "minders." Pretend that you are a reporter covering the war, either embedded or unilateral, and write a news story about your imaginary experiences.

Prior to the 2003 invasion of Iraq, many U.S. government officials believed that the Iraqi people would welcome coalition troops and be grateful to them for removing Saddam Hussein from power. Instead, many Iraqis expressed mixed feelings about the invasion, and the coalition troops faced fierce resistance in many areas of Iraq. Imagine that you are an Iraqi citizen in March 2003 and American troops have just entered your town. How do you react? Do you help the troops, fight them, or hide from them? How does your answer change depending on your religion, ethnic background, and the region of Iraq in which you live? Write a one-page essay explaining your answers.

Once the 2003 Iraq War ended, the Coalition Provisional Authority faced a number of difficult challenges in reconstructing postwar Iraq. For example, they had to rebuild schools, hospitals, and other facilities that were damaged in the war; restore electricity and water supplies; provide humanitarian aid to the Iraqi people; maintain security in the face of Iraqi resistance and attacks by foreign terrorists; establish an Iraqi police force; oversee the formation of a democratic government; prevent conflict between Iraq's various religious and ethnic groups; and restore Iraq's oil production capabilities. As a class, make a list of the issues involved in the reconstruction process. If you were in the position of U.S. civil administrator L. Paul Bremer III, how would you prioritize these issues? Create your own plan or timeline for Iraq's reconstruction and transition to democracy.

Background of the Conflict

In August 1990 the Middle Eastern country of Iraq invaded the nation of Kuwait, its smaller neighbor to the south. In early 1991 the United States joined forces with a number of other countries in Operation Desert Storm, with the goal of pushing the Iraqi army out of Kuwait. Since both Iraq and Kuwait are located at the northern tip of a body of water called the Persian Gulf, this conflict became known as the Persian Gulf War. The Persian Gulf War ended in a dramatic victory for the U.S.-led coalition in February 1991, when Iraqi troops were forced to withdraw from Kuwait after six weeks of fighting.

The United Nations (UN) agreement that officially ended the Persian Gulf War required Iraq to destroy or remove all of its biological, chemical, and nuclear weapons. In the decade after the war ended, however, Iraqi President Saddam Hussein (1937–) consistently refused to meet the terms of this peace agreement. The international community tried a number of different approaches to persuade Hussein to cooperate with UN weapons inspectors, including diplomatic negotiations, economic sanctions (trade restrictions intended to punish a country for violating international law), and military strikes. Finally, in early 2003 the United States launched a second war against Iraq, which became known as the Iraq War or Gulf War II. This military action, code named Operation Iraqi Freedom, succeeded in removing Hussein from power.

The early history of the Arab world

The roots of these two modern wars go back centuries, to the early history of the Arab world. The people known as Arabs live primarily in North Africa and the Middle East. They live in a number of different countries, from Sudan and Somalia in Africa to Egypt, Syria, Saudi Arabia, and Iraq in the Middle East. The main factor connecting the Arabs in these different countries is that they all speak the Arabic language. Although some Arabic speakers use different dialects (local versions of a language), the written form of the language is the same across the Arab world. This common language creates a shared culture among Arabs and helps them feel like a single, united group.

Most Arabs are Muslims, meaning that they practice a religion known as Islam. Muslims worship one god, called Allah. They believe that Allah revealed himself to man through the Koran, a holy book written in Arabic. The prophet Muhammad (c. 570–632) founded Islam and began spreading Allah's word in the year 622 C.E. (In Islam, a prophet is a man chosen by Allah to be his messenger to the world.) Over the next few centuries Muslims divided into two main branches, Sunni and Shiite. The two groups differ mainly over which prophets they consider the rightful successors to Muhammad. About 90 percent of all Muslims are Sunnis. Today the religion of Islam is practiced by roughly one billion people around the world. It is the principal religion in large parts of Asia, Africa, and the Middle East.

But not all Arabs are Muslims, and not all Muslims are Arabs. The Arab world also includes some Christians who are considered Arabs because they speak Arabic. In addition, many people who practice the religion of Islam do not speak Arabic. Even some Muslim countries in the Middle East are not part of the Arab world. For example, two of Iraq's close neighbors, Turkey and Iran, are Muslim countries that are not considered Arab because most of their people speak a different language (Turkish and Persian, respectively).

Ancient Mesopotamia and the Ottoman Empire

The area of the Middle East that is now known as Iraq was the site of one of the world's first great civilizations. It was called Mesopotamia, which means "land between the rivers" in Greek, because it was located in the fertile plain between the Tigris and Euphrates Rivers. By 2500 B.C.E. Mesopotamia was the center of political activity in the region. The city of Baghdad, situated on the banks of the Tigris River, was the heart of Mesopotamia. It was one of the world's great cities and eventually became the cultural center of Islam. (Baghdad now serves as the capital of modern Iraq.)

An engraving of the prophet Muhammad receiving his call from Allah to found the Islamic religion. *©Corbis. Reproduced by permission.*

Around 1500 B.C.E. Mesopotamia came under the control of the Ottoman Empire. The Ottomans were non-Arab Turks who had adopted the religion of Islam. Based in Constantinople (which later became the city of Istanbul in Turkey), these invaders wanted to control the Arab world. Once they had conquered Mesopotamia, the Ottomans divided the region into three provinces based on the ethnic and religious differences of the people who lived there. The Mosul Province in the north was populated mostly by Kurds, a non-Arab people with their own distinct culture and traditions. The central Baghdad Province was controlled by Sunni Muslims, while the Basra Province in the south was held by Shiite Muslims. After seizing Mesopotamia, the Ottomans gradually expanded their rule over much of the Middle East. The rulers of the sheikhdom of Kuwait, the Sabah family, agreed to become part of the Ottoman Empire in 1871. (A sheikhdom is a small state ruled by a sheikh, or Arab chieftain.) The Ottomans then joined Kuwait to the Basra Province.

During the late 1800s Great Britain began taking an interest in the Middle East. The British Empire had expanded to include India, and British leaders saw valuable opportunities for trade in the Persian Gulf region to the west of India. At the same time, the power of the Ottoman Empire had begun to weaken. More and more countries under its control were beginning to press for independence. Kuwait's Sabah family formed a trade relationship with the British that grew into a formal alliance as the Ottomans lost their hold on the region. In 1899 Sheik Mubarak Sabah (1837–1915; ruled 1896–1915) signed an agreement that made Kuwait a protectorate (a dependent political unit) of Great Britain. In exchange, the British gave the Sabah family a large sum of money. The Ottomans never formally recognized the agreement, however, and continued to treat Kuwait as a semi-independent part of their empire.

European rule in the Middle East

When World War I (1914–18) broke out, the Ottoman Empire sided with Germany against the Allied powers, which included Great Britain, France, Russia, Japan, and the United States. After the Allies won the war in 1918, Great Britain and France largely divided the defeated Ottoman Empire between themselves. By 1920 Turkey was the only territory that remained under Ottoman control. The British maintained control of Kuwait, which had sided with the Allies during the war. They also took charge of the areas that would become Iraq and Saudi Arabia.

In 1921 British leaders met with Middle Eastern leaders at the Cairo Conference in Egypt. The purpose of this meeting was to determine the boundaries of the new countries that would be formed in the areas under British control. The following year Great Britain sent a representative to Baghdad, High Commissioner Sir Percy Cox (1864–1937). Cox established the modern borders of Iraq, Saudi Arabia, and Kuwait. He also installed leaders in these new countries who he believed would be loyal to Great Britain and support British interests.

Although they were not completely happy with Cox's decisions, the leaders of Kuwait and Saudi Arabia accepted the new borders. But the leaders of Iraq were angered by the boundaries the British government had established for their country. One of their main complaints was that they had received only 36 miles (58 kilometers) of coastline on the Persian Gulf. Furthermore, this coastline did not feature a good location for a commercial port. Iraqi leaders felt that their limited access to the Persian Gulf would seriously affect their country's potential for trade.

Another major Iraqi complaint centered on the fact that the British had created the country by combining three former Ottoman provinces—Mosul, Baghdad, and Basra. These provinces were home to different ethnic and religious groups that would not necessarily have chosen to live together under a single government. Some Iraqis felt that the British had created an "artificial state" without regard for the people who lived there.

Sir Percy Cox established the modern borders of Iraq, Saudi Arabia, and Kuwait while these countries were under British control in 1921. ©Corbis. Reproduced by permission.

Finally, Iraqi leaders pointed out that Kuwait had been a part of Basra Province under the Ottoman Empire. They argued that Kuwait should therefore be part of Iraq. They felt that the British had taken away land that lawfully belonged to them. The Iraqi interest in Kuwait was increased by the fact that Kuwait possessed a coastline that stretched 310 miles (499 kilometers) along the Persian Gulf.

The effects of European rule over the Middle East can still be felt today. Some Arabs resent the tiny Gulf sheikhdoms—such as Kuwait, Oman, Qatar, Bahrain, and United Arab Emirates—that were created under British rule. They view these countries as artificial states that were created to serve European interests. They feel that the creation of these states unjustly divided the Arab world and led to political tensions across the region. In fact, some Arabs want to erase the national borders dividing the countries of the Middle East and unite the Arab world under a single government.

A map of the Middle East. These modern borders were established while the region was under British rule during the early 1920s. *Map by XNR Productions, Inc. Thomson Gale. Reproduced by permission.*

Such feelings played a role in Iraq's 1990 invasion of Kuwait, which in turn led to the 1991 Persian Gulf War.

Iraq becomes an independent nation

Iraq gained its independence from British rule in 1932. Over the next few decades, Iraqi leaders made several attempts—both peaceful and forceful—to gain control of Kuwait. For example, Iraq's first ruler, King Faisal I (1885–1933; ruled

1921–33), proposed that Iraq be united with Kuwait shortly after Iraq became independent. But Kuwait was still a British protectorate at the time, and both the British government and Kuwait's ruling Sabah family rejected Faisal's idea.

In 1958 Iraq's monarchy was overthrown in a bloody military uprising. Three years later Kuwait declared its independence from British rule. As soon as British troops withdrew from Kuwait in 1961, however, Iraq's military ruler, General Abdul Karim Qassem (1914–1963; ruled 1958–63) again tried to claim Kuwait. Qassem sent troops to the Kuwaiti border, but he was forced to pull them back when the British military rushed back to defend Kuwait. The British troops that protected Kuwait from Iraqi invasion were eventually replaced by Arab League forces. Founded in 1945, the Arab League is an alliance of about twenty Arab nations that promotes political, military, and economic cooperation in the Arab world.

Iraqi military ruler General Abdul Karim Qassem tried to claim Kuwait as Iraqi territory in 1961. *Getty Images. Reproduced by permission.*

In 1963 Qassem's government was overthrown by the Baath Party. The Baath Party was founded in the 1940s to support the idea of reuniting the Arab world as one powerful nation. One of its members was a young revolutionary named Saddam Hussein, who would eventually become the president of Iraq. The Baath Party only held on to power for nine months before it was overthrown. But it returned to power in 1968, led by General Ahmed Hassan al-Bakr (1914–1982; ruled 1968–79), Hussein's older cousin.

The new Iraqi government formally recognized Kuwait's independence in exchange for a payment of $85 million from the Kuwaiti government. But Bakr and his followers refused to settle on a specific border between Iraq and Kuwait. One factor in this ongoing border dispute was the South Rumaila oil field. This valuable oil reserve was squarely in the border region, and both countries wanted control over it. In 1973 Iraq once again marched its troops to the Kuwaiti border but withdrew under pressure from the Arab League. But this would not be the final time that Iraq threatened to take its smaller neighbor by force. In 1990 Iraq at last followed through on its threat.

Saddam Hussein's Rise to Power

The main figure on the Iraqi side of the 1991 Persian Gulf War was Saddam Hussein (1937–; ruled 1979–2003). After becoming president of Iraq in 1979, Hussein involved his country in two major wars over the next dozen years. The story of Hussein's youth and his rise to power helps explain his aggressive behavior toward his neighbors in the Middle East.

Saddam Hussein, whose name means "he who confronts" in Arabic, was born in 1937. He grew up as a peasant near the Sunni Muslim village of Tikrit, which is located about 100 miles (161 kilometers) north of Baghdad along the Tigris River. After he came to power, Hussein invented or exaggerated many details of his early life to enhance his image as a powerful and ruthless leader. As a result, some facts about his life are uncertain.

It is known that Hussein's father either died or left the family before Saddam was born. The main influences in his young life were his stepfather and one of his uncles. Hussein has said that he endured a difficult childhood, in which he was abused and often prevented from attending school. Some historians claim that his harsh upbringing taught him to view other people with mistrust and to rely only upon himself. Hussein also realized at a young age that threats and violence would help him get what he wanted. He has claimed that he was ten years old when he first killed someone. It is known that when he was a teenager, Hussein killed his brother-in-law during a violent family argument and was sent to prison for six months.

The Baath Party

In 1957, as a twenty-year-old student, Hussein joined the Iraqi Baath Party. (*Baath* means "rebirth" or "renaissance" in Arabic.) Baathism was a radical political movement founded in the 1940s by Syrian revolutionary Michel Aflaq (1910–1989). The idea behind the movement was to unite the Arab world and create one powerful Arab state. The Iraqi Baath Party was a small, disorganized splinter group of this larger movement. It was made up primarily of violent and ruthless men who were willing to do anything to take control of the Iraqi government.

In 1959 Hussein was one of a group of Baath revolutionaries who tried to murder Iraq's military ruler, General Abdul Karim Qassem (1914–1963). When the assassination attempt failed, Hussein left Iraq in order to avoid capture. He fled to Syria and eventually settled in Cairo, Egypt, where he entered a university and studied law. In 1963 the Baath Party succeeded in overthrowing the Iraqi government. Hussein immediately returned to Iraq and claimed his place in the new regime. Thanks to the support of his older cousin, Ahmed Hassan al-Bakr (1914–1982), Hussein was given a position in the Baath regional command, which was the party's highest decision-making body in Iraq.

As soon as it gained control of the government, the Baath Party showed Iraqi citizens that it was willing to use violence and threats to remain in power. First, it proved that the former leaders would not be returning by showing Qassem's dead body on Iraqi television. A Baath Party official pointed out the bullet holes in the corpse and then spat into the murdered general's face. Over the next few months the Baathists turned Iraq's royal palace into a torture chamber for their enemies. Some prisoners who survived later testified that they had been questioned and tortured by Hussein himself.

The Iraqi military managed to overthrow the Baathists and regain control of the government less than a year later. The military rulers threw Hussein and several other Baath Party leaders in prison. Hussein used his time in captivity to think about why his party had failed to stay in power. He felt that party leaders had placed too much trust in the Iraqi military to support them. He decided to build his own security force within the party so that the Baathists would not have to depend on the military to regain power. Hussein escaped from prison after two years and became the security organizer for the Baath Party. He created a large force that used violence to terrify citizens and remove rival political leaders.

In 1968 the Baath Party again overthrew the Iraqi government and returned to power. Bakr became president of Iraq, and his ambitious younger cousin Hussein became deputy chairman of the party's Revolutionary Command Council. Hussein also served as the head of internal security for the Baathist government. Controlling the forces that helped the party maintain power through threats and violence, Hussein became the most powerful person in the government. He forged close relationships with other party leaders during this time, but he later betrayed many of these men to further his own career.

A young Saddam Hussein, who quickly rose through the ranks of the Baath Party. *AP/Wide World Photos. Reproduced by permission.*

Although the Baathist government kept many of its violent activities secret, it also sometimes used public displays of force to keep its critics in line. For example, in January 1969 Iraq arrested a number of foreign journalists and accused them of being spies for Israel. (Israel is a Jewish state in the Middle East that has a history of strained relations with many countries in the Arab world.) Seventeen of the journalists—eleven of whom were Jewish—were convicted in public trials and put to death by hanging. The executions were carried out in Liberation Square in Baghdad in front of a crowd of thousands of Iraqis.

Despite the Baathist government's brutal reputation and its disregard for human rights, Iraq still enjoyed the support of the United States and many European nations during this time. This friendly attitude was due to the fact that the United States and the Soviet Union (along with their allies) were locked in an economic and military rivalry known as the Cold War. During the Cold War, which lasted from the 1940s until 1991, U.S. foreign policy focused on preventing the communist form of government practiced in the Soviet Union from spreading to other countries. (In communism the government controls all property and industry, and goods and money are in theory shared equally among all citizens.) The United States viewed the Baath movement, with its focus on Arab nationalism (the goal of uniting the Arab world to form one powerful nation), as a good alternative to communism. The U.S. government wanted to stay on good terms with Iraq in order to maintain its influence in the Middle East, which was located directly south of the Soviet Union.

Hussein takes control of Iraq

Hussein spent the 1970s gradually getting rid of Bakr's supporters and his own rivals within the Baath Party. In July 1979 he finally managed to force his cousin out of office and seize control of the government. Shortly after becoming president of Iraq, Hussein tightened his grip on power by carrying out a bloody rampage that resulted in the deaths of an estimated five hundred people. These included military officers, Baath Party officials, and even some of Hussein's close friends and associates. At one point, Hussein presided over an event that was broadcast on Iraqi television. He ordered twenty leading citizens to read "confessions" of crimes against the government and then had them taken outside and shot as traitors.

Hussein used these brutal acts to inspire loyalty among the Iraqi people and ensure his absolute control of the government. He realized that Iraq faced both external threats from neighboring countries and internal conflicts among its different ethnic and religious groups. Hussein re-

sponded to these tensions by using violence to maintain his hold on power and make himself appear to be a strong leader who could guide the country through its problems. "I know that there are scores of people plotting to kill me," he said shortly after becoming president in 1979, as quoted in *Understanding the Crisis in the Persian Gulf* by historian Peter Cipkowski. "And this is not difficult to understand. After all, did we not seize power by plotting against our predecessors [the political leaders who came before]? Fortunately, I am far cleverer than they. I know who is conspiring to kill me long before they can actually start planning to do it. This enables me to get them before they have the slightest chance of striking at me."

Another way in which Hussein tried to look like a strong leader was by placing pictures of himself all over Baghdad. For example, his portrait appeared on the sides of buses and buildings and in every village, school, hospital, and government office. He wanted Iraqi citizens to feel his

An armored car stands outside the Presidential palace in Baghdad, Iraq, after the Baath Party overthrew the Iraqi government in 1968. *©Corbis. Reproduced by permission.*

presence in their daily lives and believe that there was no alternative to his rule.

The war with Iran

Hussein promised Iraqis that the 1980s would be a "glorious decade," during which they would restore the honor of their nation's historic past. He planned to make Iraq the most powerful country in the Middle East and himself the recognized leader of the Arab world. The first step in Hussein's plan involved attacking Iran, Iraq's neighbor to the east. Iran was a non-Arab state that had recently been torn apart by revolution. A group of Islamic fundamentalists (people who emphasize strict obedience to a set of religious principles) led by a religious leader called the Ayatollah Khomeini (1900–1989) had overthrown the government in 1979. (*Ayatollah* is a title given to respected religious leaders.) Khomeini was a Shiite Muslim and an outspoken opponent of Hussein and his Sunni Muslim government. (Sunni and Shiite are the two main branches of Islam. About 90 percent of all Muslims are Sunnis.) Although Iran was larger than Iraq and had three times as many people, Hussein believed that his highly trained armed forces could quickly defeat his enemy.

Iraq launched its invasion of Iran in September 1980. Hussein's first goal was to take control of the Shatt al Arab waterway. This important access route to the Persian Gulf begins where the Tigris and Euphrates Rivers join and forms part of the border between Iraq and Iran. The two countries had signed a formal agreement to share the waterway in 1975, but they still had clashes over it. To Hussein's surprise, the Iraqi invasion met with fierce resistance. His troops were pushed back, and he was soon forced to ask the United Nations to negotiate a cease-fire agreement. But Khomeini refused to accept the cease-fire and vowed to continue fighting his Sunni enemies. The Iran-Iraq War went on for eight long years, which were marked by nearly constant fighting along the 730-mile (1,175-kilometer) border between the two countries.

International reaction to the war

U.S. President Ronald Reagan (1911–; served 1981–89) supported Iraq during the war. He and other Amer-

A picture of Iraqi President Saddam Hussein stands at the entrance of the Doura refinery on the outskirts of Baghdad. By placing pictures of himself all over Baghdad, Hussein thought he looked like a stronger leader. *Photograph by Jockel Finck. AP/Wide World Photos. Reproduced by permission.*

ican leaders were worried that the religious fundamentalism of Iran's government might spread throughout the Middle East. They also hoped that their support would prevent Hussein from forming a close relationship with the Soviet Union, the United States' Cold War rival. At first the U.S. government only provided secret support to Iraq. In 1984, however, the United States showed the world which side it was on by establishing full diplomatic relations with Iraq.

Kuwait, Iraq's small neighbor to the south, also sided with Iraq. Kuwait's government, like Iraq's, was controlled by Sunni Muslims who wanted to prevent Iran's Shiites from gaining too much power in the region. The Kuwaiti government loaned billions of dollars to Iraq during the war.

During the war, Hussein's troops used chemical weapons against Iranian troops on several occasions. Iraqi forces fired artillery shells containing either mustard gas (a blistering agent that can cause blindness or death) or Tabun (a deadly nerve gas) at the enemy. The use of these and other chemical and biological weapons was outlawed under a series of international treaties known as the Geneva Conventions. The conventions were developed in Geneva, Switzerland, between 1864 and 1949. They are intended to guarantee the humane treatment of enemy soldiers and prisoners and the protection of civilians (people not involved in the fighting, including women and children) during wartime.

The governments of the United States and many other countries did not approve of the fact that Iraq had broken international law by using chemical weapons. But most were reluctant to become involved—partly because some of the weapons Iraq used had been developed with the help of American and European scientists.

The end of the conflict

Toward the end of 1986 Iran announced its "last campaign," which it predicted would bring the war to an end by the following year. In December 1986 Iranian forces tried to capture a small island in the Shatt al Arab waterway. They planned to use this island to stage an assault on the city of Basra in southern Iraq. But the Iraqi forces successfully defended Basra and caused seventy thousand enemy casualties (killed and wounded soldiers) while suffering only ten thousand casualties themselves. It was a major defeat for Iran.

In early 1988 Iraq went on the offensive and launched an all-out air war against Iran. The Iraqi air force dropped bombs that destroyed several important energy-production facilities in Iran. Meanwhile, the Iraqi army fired more than one hundred Soviet-built missiles called Scuds into the Iranian capital city of Tehran. Finally, Hus-

sein launched a ground war and captured some Iranian territory. Iranian citizens began to believe that Khomeini could not protect them, and feelings of resentment about the long war grew stronger. With his people angry and his army weakened, Khomeini finally accepted a cease-fire in July 1988.

As soon as Hussein's troops returned home, he turned them against his own people. The non-Arab Kurds of northern Iraq had spent decades struggling to gain their independence and establish a homeland. Some Kurdish groups had supported Iran during the war. Hussein viewed the Kurds as a group of rebels who posed a threat to his rule. The Iraqi army attacked Kurdish villages with chemical weapons in 1988, killing thousands of people. An estimated 250,000 Kurds fled Iraq, becoming refugees in Turkey and Iran. Although many nations criticized Iraq for using chemical weapons against the Kurds, once again they did not take any official action against Hussein for violating international law.

Though Hussein's army won the war against Iran, the eight-year conflict left the Iraqi economy in ruins. Iraq spent an estimated $500 billion to fight the war, and by the time it ended, Iraq owed $80 billion to other countries. Throughout the war years Hussein had spent massive amounts of money on modern weapons and equipment. He also recruited approximately one million troops, which gave him the fourth-largest army in the world (after the Soviet Union, China, and the United States). Finally, he built relationships with the leaders of both the United States and the Soviet Union. But while the Iran-Iraq War had left Hussein with a tough, battle-hardened, and well-equipped military, he still lacked money to help his country recover from the war. With this in mind, he decided to use his fearsome army to invade Iraq's rich neighbors, Kuwait and Saudi Arabia, and claim their wealth for his own.

U.S.-Iraqi relations and Hussein's miscalculations

The time between the end of the Iran-Iraq War in 1988 and Iraq's invasion of Kuwait in 1990 was filled with mixed messages and misunderstandings. As Hussein prepared to attack Kuwait, he tried to predict how the world would respond. He came to believe, given their history of inaction, that the United States and other Western powers would not get involved. At the same time, world leaders misunderstood Hussein's intentions. They never thought that he would start another war so soon after the damaging and expensive Iran-Iraq War. In an effort to maintain friendly relations with Iraq, they overlooked many signs of Hussein's plans.

For example, the United States and other countries did not approve of Iraq using chemical weapons against the Kurds. Hussein was strongly criticized in the international media, but very little was done. In fact, official U.S. policy referred to the situation as "an internal matter" for Iraq. The U.S. government also received reports from the human-rights organization Amnesty International documenting human-rights abuses in Iraq. These reports claimed that the Iraqi government routinely killed political opponents and even tortured children in order to force information from their parents. Still, the U.S.

State Department sent official New Year's greetings to Iraq in January 1990 and expressed its desire to further develop the friendship between the two countries.

Threats and negotiations

Over the next few months, Hussein began making threats against other countries in the Middle East. For example, Hussein warned that he would not hesitate to use chemical weapons if Israel ever attacked Iraq. Many people around the world were outraged by Saddam's threat, and some governments considered using economic sanctions (trade restrictions and other measures designed to hurt a country's economy) to punish him for his statement. Instead the U.S. government sent a group of legislators to Baghdad in April 1990 to meet with the Iraqi leader. The group included Senator Robert Dole (1923–) of Kansas, Senator Howard Metzenbaum (1917–) of Ohio, and Senator Alan Simpson (1931–) of Wyoming.

Iraqi Kurds hold photos of victims of the Iraqi army attack on Halabja in 1998. Halabja is the city where more than four thousand Kurds were killed in a poison gas attack by the Iraqi army. *Photograph by Hasan Karbakhshian. AP/Wide World Photos. Reproduced by permission.*

The Iraqi government released a transcript of parts of the meeting, which later aired on American television. Based on this transcript, the meeting seemed friendly and professional. Members of the American delegation later insisted that they had expressed grave concerns about Hussein's aggressive statements, but these comments did not appear in the Iraqi record of the meeting. Instead, the transcript made it appear that the United States would remain on the sidelines if Iraq followed through on its threats.

In July 1990 Hussein threatened to use force against any Middle Eastern country that pumped excess oil. Many countries in the Middle East, including Iraq and Kuwait, contain some of the world's largest underground oil reserves. These countries make money by pumping and exporting oil (selling it to other countries around the world). In 1960 the world's major oil-producing countries formed the Organization of Petroleum Exporting Countries (OPEC) in order to coordinate their oil production. OPEC sets limits, or quotas, on the amount of oil its members pump each year to ensure that oil prices remain stable. Hussein's threat was clearly aimed at Kuwait, which had been pumping more oil than was allowed under OPEC agreements. Kuwait's actions contributed to a decline in oil prices, from $20.50 per barrel in early 1990 to $13.60 per barrel in July. Every dollar drop in the price per barrel cost Iraq an estimated $1 billion per year. Hussein thus blamed Kuwait for making Iraq's financial problems worse.

On July 17 Hussein made a fiery speech in which he accused Kuwait of stealing oil from the Iraqi side of the South Rumaila oil field, which straddled the border of Iraq and Kuwait. "The oil quota violators have stabbed Iraq with a poison dagger," he declared, as quoted in *Understanding the Crisis in the Persian Gulf.* "Iraqis will not forget the saying that cutting necks is better than cutting means of living. Oh, God Almighty, be witness that we have warned them!"

At this point Hussein began moving Iraqi troops toward the Kuwaiti border. He also ordered that groups of missiles be aimed at Kuwait and Israel. Although U.S. government officials were concerned, they seemed to think that Hussein was bluffing. They did not strongly criticize Iraq's actions or directly state that they would protect Kuwait if it were attacked. For example, when asked about a potential

Iraqi invasion of Kuwait, U.S. State Department spokesperson Margaret Tutwiler explained that the United States had no defense treaties with Kuwait. This meant that the United States was under no obligation to aid Kuwait if it came under attack.

On July 25 the U.S. ambassador to Iraq, April Glaspie (1942–), held a meeting with Hussein. The Iraqi government released a partial transcript of the meeting that quoted Glaspie as saying, "We [the U.S. government] have no opinion on the Arab-Arab conflicts, like your border disagreements with Kuwait." Glaspie later claimed that Iraqi officials had removed parts of the discussion from the transcript. She said that she had also warned Hussein that the United States would insist on the conflict being settled peacefully and would defend Kuwait against an Iraqi attack. Hussein either misunderstood or chose to ignore such statements. Although the United States repeatedly expressed concern about Iraq's aggressive behavior, Hussein came to believe that the U.S. government would not send troops to protect Kuwait. He became convinced that the only punishment he would receive for invading Kuwait would be an international scolding.

In the meantime, some of Iraq's Arab neighbors also expressed concern about Hussein's threats and troop movements toward Kuwait. President Hosni Mubarak (1928–) of Egypt and King Hussein (1935–1999; ruled 1953–99) of Jordan (no relation to Saddam Hussein) arranged diplomatic talks in an attempt to help Iraq and Kuwait resolve their differences. High-ranking Kuwaiti and Iraqi officials met in Saudi Arabia on July 31. During these talks, Iraq threatened to invade Kuwait unless the Kuwaiti government met a series of demands.

First, Iraq demanded that Kuwait forgive Iraq of its war debts. Kuwait had loaned Iraq billions of dollars during the Iran-Iraq War. Iraq argued that it should not have to repay this money because it had fought Iran in order to protect all Arab interests in the Persian Gulf. Second, Iraq insisted that Kuwait limit its future oil production to ensure high oil prices in world markets. Finally, Iraq demanded that Kuwait give up possession of the island of Bubiyan in the Persian Gulf. This large island off the southern coast of Iraq would provide Hussein with a strategic port on the Gulf.

Kuwait made some attempts to meet these demands. For example, Kuwaiti leaders agreed to limit their country's production of oil. OPEC then stepped in and announced an increase in the price its member countries would charge for oil, which would help Iraq's troubled economy. Kuwaiti negotiators indicated they were willing to continue discussing Iraq's other conditions. In the meantime, however, Hussein continued sending troops to the Kuwaiti border. Some estimates put the number of Iraqi forces gathered along the border at one hundred thousand troops. On August 2, 1990, to the shock of many people in the Middle East and around the world, Iraq announced the postponement of future peace talks and launched its invasion of Kuwait.

Iraq Invades Kuwait

After months of political discussions and military buildup, Iraq launched its invasion of Kuwait on August 2, 1990, at 2 AM The powerful Iraqi military successfully conquered its smaller neighbor in a matter of hours. Nations around the world condemned the invasion and demanded that Iraq immediately withdraw its troops from Kuwait. Although Iraqi President Saddam Hussein (1937–) was surprised by the world's strong reaction, he refused to remove his forces and instead began threatening nearby Saudi Arabia. The United States and many other countries began sending troops into the Middle East to defend Saudi Arabia and, if necessary, force Iraq to withdraw from Kuwait. This created a tense military standoff that lasted for six months before finally erupting into the Persian Gulf War.

Iraq invades Kuwait

When more than 100,000 highly trained Iraqi troops began pouring across the border into Kuwait on August 2, there was little doubt that they would achieve their goal of capturing the capital, Kuwait City. The tiny country of

Kuwait was completely outmatched. Before the Persian Gulf War, Iraq had a land area of 170,000 square miles (440,000 square kilometers) and a population of around 18 million. Its army consisted of 1 million men and a variety of modern weapons and equipment. On the other hand, Kuwait had a land area of only 7,000 square miles (18,130 square kilometers, or about the size of the state of New Jersey) and a population of around 2 million. Less than 20,000 men were on active duty in the Kuwaiti army.

As the invasion began, columns of Iraqi tanks sped down the six-lane highway leading toward Kuwait City, located about 80 miles (130 kilometers) south of the Iraqi border. They met with almost no resistance along the way. Upon learning that the Iraqi army was approaching, the emir (ruler) of Kuwait, Prince Jaber al-Ahmed al-Sabah, left the country by boat in the middle of the night. He fled to Saudi Arabia along with the heir to the throne, Prince Saad al-Abdullah al-Sabah, and the rest of Kuwait's royal family. The following morning, Prince Saad appeared on Saudi television to tell the world that Kuwait would fight until it regained its territory.

The taking of Kuwait City

By this time, however, the Iraqi forces were well on their way to capturing Kuwait City. Unlike the royal family, most Kuwaitis had no advance warning of the invasion. In fact, many only learned about it when they awoke to find Iraqi tanks rumbling through the streets. The early daylight hours of August 2 were a time of confusion and chaos in Kuwait City. Many residents reported hearing gunfire and explosions and seeing helicopters and military jets flying overhead. A U.S. Army officer happened to be staying at the Kuwait International Hotel that morning. "I looked out my window and saw flashes across the horizon," Major John F. Feeley Jr. recalled in *The Persian Gulf War* by Zachary Kent. "It was like lightning, except it was coming from the wrong direction. It was coming from the ground up."

Some Kuwaiti army units organized a limited response to the surprise attack, but they were quickly overrun by Iraq's invasion forces. A few Kuwaiti citizens also tried to fight back, but they too were brushed aside by Iraq's powerful army. As Iraqi troops approached the royal palace, the

emir's brother, Sheik Fahd, and some of his personal guards stood on the steps with their pistols drawn and tried to prevent the Iraqis from entering. But Iraqi soldiers shot and killed them after a brief battle.

By midmorning the Iraqi forces had captured all of their main targets in Kuwait City. They had taken control of the royal palace, key government offices, the central bank where Kuwait's gold reserves were stored, and the Kuwaiti television and radio stations. The invasion had taken a total of seven hours. Hussein ordered thirty thousand troops to occupy Kuwait City. The remaining Iraqi forces continued moving south through Kuwait toward the border of Saudi Arabia.

Iraqi soldiers in a military transport truck in a street of Kuwait City after Iraq invaded Kuwait in August 1990. *AFP Photo/Kuna. Reproduced by permission.*

The world responds

U.S. President George H. W. Bush (1924–; served 1989–93) learned about Iraq's invasion of Kuwait shortly after it began from officials at the American embassy in Kuwait City. The U.S. government released a statement condemning the invasion and calling for the immediate withdrawal of Iraqi forces from Kuwait. Later in the day, Bush discussed the situation in a news conference and declared that there was "no place in today's world for this sort of naked aggression." British Prime Minister Margaret Thatcher (1925–; served 1979–90), who happened to be visiting the United States at the time, also spoke out sternly against Iraq's actions. "If we let [the invasion] succeed no small country can ever feel safe again," she stated in Peter Cipkowski's *Understanding the Crisis in the Persian Gulf.* "The law of the jungle takes over."

One after another, countries around the world expressed their disapproval of the invasion. The leaders of Russia condemned the attack and called for the restoration of Kuwaiti sovereignty (freedom from external control). The Chinese government expressed its concern about the situation and encouraged both sides to find a peaceful solution. The European Community (an economic alliance of twelve European nations that later became known as the European Union) also issued a statement condemning the invasion.

The United Nations Security Council held a special meeting on August 2 to discuss the situation. Within the United Nations, the Security Council has the primary responsibility for maintaining international peace and security. The Security Council consists of five permanent members—the United States, Russia, Great Britain, France, and China—and ten elected members that each serve two-year terms. At the special meeting the Security Council passed Resolution 660. This resolution officially condemned Iraq's invasion of Kuwait, demanded the immediate withdrawal of Iraqi forces, and called for negotiations to settle the crisis. Fourteen of the fifteen Security Council members voted in favor of the resolution, while the Middle Eastern country of Yemen abstained (did not vote).

Mixed feelings in the Middle East

While much of the world disapproved of Iraq's invasion of Kuwait, the reaction in the Middle East was mixed. Several Arab states immediately spoke out against the invasion, including Morocco, Algeria, and Lebanon. But several

U.S. representative James Baker and British representative Sir G. Howe at a UN Security Council meeting regarding Iraq's invasion of Kuwait. ©J A Giordano/Corbis SABA. Reproduced by permission.

countries in the Persian Gulf region remained silent or reacted cautiously. Some of these countries, like Saudi Arabia, were shocked by Iraq's actions and worried about what Hussein might do next. King Hussein (1935–1999; ruled 1953–99) of Jordan (no relation to Saddam Hussein) wanted the Arab nations of the Middle East to work together to resolve the conflict between Iraq and Kuwait, without the involvement of the United States and other Western powers (the noncommunist countries of Western Europe and North America).

Hussein's decision to invade Kuwait was quite popular among Iraqis. It also found support in some other Arab nations, such as Sudan and Yemen. The people of these countries tended to view Kuwait and Saudi Arabia as artificial states that were created to serve Western interests. They felt that the creation of these states in the 1920s, when the Persian Gulf area was under British rule, unfairly divided the Arab world and led to political tensions across the region. Furthermore, some Arabs resented Kuwait's close ties to the

United States, which in turn was a strong supporter of their bitter enemy, Israel.

Israel had been created by the UN in 1948 as a homeland for all Jewish people. Its location in the Middle East was also the ancient homeland of an Arab people called the Palestinians. When Israel became a Jewish state, thousands of Palestinians fled and became refugees in Jordan and other neighboring countries. Some of these Palestinians formed a group called the Palestine Liberation Organization (PLO). The purpose of the PLO was to reclaim lost territory and found an independent Palestinian state. The PLO has often turned to acts of violence and terrorism in its struggle with Israel.

The Arab League—a political, economic, and military alliance of twenty Arab nations and the PLO—held a meeting to discuss the invasion of Kuwait. Fifteen members of the Arab League issued a joint statement calling for the withdrawal of Iraqi forces. But Jordan, Libya, Yemen, Sudan, Djibouti, and the PLO refused to sign the statement. While they did not necessarily support the invasion, they viewed it as an effort by Hussein to place Arab interests ahead of American and Israeli interests. A short time later, King Hussein of Jordan and PLO leader Yasir Arafat (1929–) went to Baghdad to meet with Hussein. They warned him to be cautious and presented peace plans aimed at avoiding U.S. military involvement.

Operation Desert Shield

The aim of avoiding U.S. involvement was useless, since the American military became involved within a week of the invasion. First Kuwait's ambassador to the UN, Sheik Saud Nasir al-Sabah, directly asked for U.S. military assistance to help free his country. Then, as Iraqi troops began to gather along the border of Saudi Arabia, that country's ruler, King Fahd (1923–; ruled 1982–), agreed to allow American troops to enter Saudi Arabia and help defend it against a possible invasion.

On August 8, 1990, President Bush announced that he was sending U.S. forces to Saudi Arabia. He explained that his aims were to persuade Iraq to withdraw from Kuwait, restore Kuwait's government to power, ensure the security of the Persian Gulf region, and protect American citizens in the area. "America does not seek conflict," Bush said, as quoted

in the August 9, 1990, *New York Times*. "But America will stand by her friends." He gave the military buildup the code name Operation Desert Shield. It ended up being the largest deployment of American troops overseas since the Vietnam War (1955–75).

A number of other countries began sending troops to Saudi Arabia as well. The coalition (a temporary alliance of countries working toward a common goal) against Iraq eventually included thirty-one countries, nine of which were located in the Middle East (Bahrain, Egypt, Kuwait, Morocco, Oman, Qatar, Saudi Arabia, Syria, and United Arab Emirates). But some Arab leaders criticized the participation of Arab states in the coalition. For example, King Hussein of Jordan condemned Saudi Arabia's decision to allow Western military forces to be stationed in its territory. He claimed that the United States and its allies were only interested in protecting their oil supplies, rather than in helping the people of the Middle East.

Arab leaders (from left to right), Yemeni Vice President Ali Salem Al Beedh, King Hussein of Jordan, Iraqi President Saddam Hussein, and Palestinian leader Yasir Arafat meet in Baghdad to discuss peace plans aimed at avoiding U.S. military involvement. *AP/Wide World Photos. Reproduced by permission.*

In the meantime, the UN took other steps to punish Iraq for its invasion of Kuwait. On August 6 the Security Council passed Resolution 661, which imposed economic sanctions (trade restrictions aimed at forcing a nation to obey international law) against Iraq. Eighteen countries voted in favor of the resolution, while Yemen and Cuba abstained. Following this resolution, countries around the world stopped trading with Iraq. They refused to buy oil from Iraq or to send it shipments of food, weapons, or other goods. These international actions forced Hussein to rely only on his own internal resources, which were strained from the war with Iran.

Hussein annexes Kuwait

Hussein was surprised by the strong negative response to his invasion of Kuwait. He had misread signals from U.S. government officials and convinced himself that the international community would not interfere. He never expected the countries of the world to come together against him. Hussein reacted angrily to the American military buildup in Saudi Arabia and to the economic sanctions imposed by the United Nations. At one point, according to *The March to War* by James Ridgeway, he promised to "pluck out the eyes of those who would attack the Arab nation." Hussein also said that the Iraqi people "would rather die in dignity than live in humiliation."

In the meantime, Iraq's occupying forces began organizing a new, pro-Iraqi government in Kuwait. They seized all the assets of the ruling Sabah family and announced that the emir no longer held any power in Kuwait. Then the Iraqis tried to find Kuwaiti citizens who would be willing to serve in a "transitional [temporary] free government." But the Kuwaitis realized that this government would not hold any real power. Instead, it would be a puppet administration for Hussein, doing whatever he told it to do. The Iraqis were unable to find any leading citizens willing to join the proposed government. The occupying forces later announced that they had formed a new government led by Kuwaiti officers and provided a list of names. But Kuwaiti diplomats outside the country told the world that the names all belonged to Iraqis.

On August 8 Hussein abandoned his attempt to form a transitional government in Kuwait. Instead he announced that Iraq was annexing (formally making it a part of Iraq) Kuwait. "Thank God that we are now one people, one state that will be the pride of the Arabs," Hussein stated, as quoted in *The Persian Gulf War* by Zachary Kent. But annexing Kuwait turned out to be a terrible mistake. It was the first annexation of an independent nation since Germany annexed Austria and Czechoslovakia during World War II (1939–45). It thus reminded many people of Germany's aggression under dictator Adolf Hitler (1889–1945) in that war. In addition, Iraq's annexation of Kuwait frightened many small countries around the world. If Hussein could simply take over his smaller neighbor, other powerful nations might do the same thing to them.

Hussein's annexation of Kuwait made it difficult for even his allies to defend him. On August 9 the United Nations Security Council unanimously (with the agreement of all) passed Resolution 662, which condemned the annexation and declared it null and void (refused to acknowledge it). The Arab League held an emergency meeting on August 10. Representatives from both Iraq and Kuwait attended the meeting. The Arab League also passed a resolution refusing to recognize Iraq's annexation of Kuwait. Twelve member states voted in favor of the resolution, while three voted against it and three abstained. The countries that had voted in favor of the resolution joined the coalition against Iraq and began sending troops to help protect Saudi Arabia.

Once again, Hussein was surprised by the strong international reaction. He was particularly upset at his Arab neighbors that had joined the U.S.-led coalition. He made an angry speech on Iraqi television in which he called on Arabs and Muslims everywhere to launch a *jihad,* or holy war, against the American invaders. His words generated public support in several Muslim countries, including Pakistan.

Hussein attempts to raise support

Over the next few days, Hussein took steps to increase his base of support in the Arab world. For example, Hussein knew that most Arabs supported the Palestinians in their efforts to reclaim lost territory from Israel. He also knew that many Arabs did not want the United States and other Western powers to decide issues in the Middle East. On August 12 he announced his own peace plan, which linked these popular ideas to his invasion of Kuwait. Hussein's plan called for American military forces to withdraw from Saudi Arabia and be replaced with Arab League forces. It also requested an end to the economic sanctions against Iraq. Finally, Hussein demanded that Israel withdraw from the Palestinian territories it occupied. In exchange, he offered to withdraw Iraqi troops from Kuwait. The proposal met with little interest.

A few days later, Hussein made peace with Iran, his neighbor to the north. Iraq and Iran had fought each other in an eight-year war that ended with a cease-fire in 1988. The two sides had never agreed on the terms of a peace treaty, and they continued to argue over territory that had changed hands during the war. Hussein finally agreed to terms that favored Iran to prevent it from joining the coalition against Iraq. Although Iran resumed diplomatic relations with its old enemy, it also promised to honor the UN's trade restrictions against Iraq.

Foreign citizens become "human shields"

At the time Iraq invaded Kuwait, thousands of foreign citizens were living and working in both countries. For example, there were 4,000 British citizens and 2,500 Americans in Kuwait when the invasion began. Many foreign-born workers managed to escape Iraq and Kuwait shortly after the invasion. But Iraqi military forces prevented many others from leaving, particularly Americans and Europeans. In addition, Iraqi troops captured a British Airways passenger jet that happened to land in Kuwait City on its way to India on the morning of August 2. They took all of the people onboard prisoner. During the first few weeks after the invasion, the safe release of these foreign citizens was the focus of many diplomatic efforts.

On August 18, however, Iraq announced that it would continue to serve as the "host" of the foreign citizens who had been trapped in Iraq and Kuwait at the time of the invasion. Furthermore, Iraqi officials said that they planned to use the foreigners as "human shields" to protect military

and industrial targets from attack. Iraqi forces then moved thousands of American, British, and French citizens to Baghdad and other key locations in Iraq and Kuwait. The idea was to prevent the growing coalition forces from launching an attack against Iraq for fear of killing their own citizens. But the use of civilians (people not involved in a war, including women and children) as human shields only increased the international outrage directed at Hussein.

President Bush spoke out angrily against Iraq's treatment of foreigners. "We have been reluctant to use the word 'hostage,'" he was quoted as saying in *The Persian Gulf War*. "But when Saddam Hussein offers to trade the freedom of those citizens of many nations he holds against their will in return for concessions [agreeing to meet demands], there can be little doubt that ... they are, in fact, hostages." On August 18 the UN Security Council passed Resolution 664, which demanded the immediate release of all foreign citizens from Iraq and Kuwait.

U.S. President George Bush, Defense Secretary Dick Cheney (left), and Chairman of the Joint Chiefs of Staff Colin Powell (right) talk with reporters regarding the Middle East situation. *Photograph by Doug Mills. AP/Wide World Photos. Reproduced by permission.*

On August 23 Hussein appeared on Iraqi television along with several of his Western hostages. The Iraqi president tried to appear friendly, even tousling the hair of one small boy. He also praised their bravery and thanked them for their role in maintaining peace. Once again, however, Hussein had miscalculated. This public appearance with his foreign prisoners created a huge outcry around the world.

At the same time, a number of well-known politicians and public figures from around the world—including American civil-rights leader Jesse Jackson (1941–), former boxer and Muslim peace activist Muhammad Ali (1942–), and former German chancellor and Nobel Peace Prize-winner Willy Brandt (1913–1992)—traveled to Baghdad to try to win the freedom of their countrymen. Hussein eventually agreed to release some of the women and children he had been holding, but he continued to use the men as human shields.

Iraq's brutal occupation of Kuwait

During the weeks following Iraq's invasion of Kuwait, the Iraqi armed forces treated the Kuwaitis terribly. As the world criticized Hussein and sent military assistance to Saudi Arabia, thousands of people in Kuwait were arrested, tortured, and killed. Iraqi soldiers randomly took civilians off the streets of Kuwait City and held them for questioning. Anyone who was suspected of resisting Iraqi rule was executed. For example, twenty-one Kuwait University professors were murdered for refusing to replace a portrait of the emir of Kuwait with one of Hussein. Many witnesses reported that the Iraqi forces set up "torture centers" to frighten and extract information from the Kuwaiti people. Initial reports also claimed that Iraqi soldiers strolled into hospitals and disconnected the incubators that were supporting premature babies. However, this claim was later retracted.

The Iraqi troops also did a great deal of physical damage to Kuwaiti property during the occupation. For example, they broke into thousands of private homes and businesses and stole everything of value, including computers, generators, hospital equipment, televisions, clothing, jewelry, and food. Many of these goods were shipped back to Iraq. They

also broke into a Kuwaiti art museum and either stole or destroyed a valuable collection of Islamic art. Iraqi soldiers even broke into the Kuwaiti National Zoo. They sent some of the more valuable animals back to Baghdad and used others for target practice or for food.

In the face of such terror and destruction, more than 1.5 million people fled the region during the months leading up to the Persian Gulf War. Many of the people who escaped were foreign-born workers from Egypt, India, and Asia. Most made their way to Saudi Arabia and Jordan. The International Red Cross, an organization that helps victims of war, set up camps in Jordan to provide food and shelter for roughly 750,000 refugees.

Some Kuwaiti citizens formed a secret resistance movement to fight the Iraqi occupation. Some resistance fighters hung anti-Iraqi banners from high buildings in Kuwait City. Others used tactics of guerrilla warfare against the Iraqis. For example, Kuwaiti guerrillas launched attacks against the Iraqi

Iraqi President Saddam Hussein appearing on television with child hostages. *©Corbis Sygma. Reproduced by permission.*

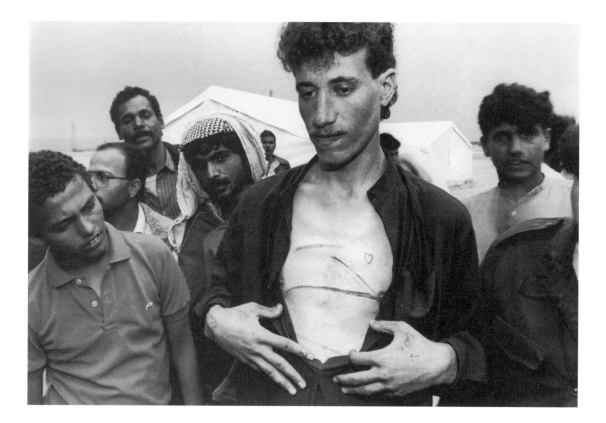

Refugees at a camp near Safwan, Iraq, look at the scars on the chest of Najwat Abdul-Razaq. Abdul-Razaq said that he was taken prisoner shortly after the Iraqi invasion of Kuwait and tortured with a razor blade by Iraqi soldiers for allegedly stealing a car. *AP/Wide World Photos. Reproduced by permission.*

embassy in Kuwait City and claimed to have shot down several Iraqi helicopters. Overall, though, the Kuwaiti resistance had little effect on the Iraqi military. In fact, some people claimed that it only made the Iraqi forces behave more brutally toward Kuwaitis. If Kuwait hoped to be free of Iraq's occupation, the tiny nation would need outside help.

The United States and Its Allies Prepare for War

4

When Iraqi President Saddam Hussein (1937–) ordered the Iraqi military to invade Kuwait in August 1990, he set in motion a series of events that would soon lead to war. Countries around the world condemned the invasion and demanded that Iraq withdraw from Kuwait. The United States led a coalition of thirty other nations that began sending troops, aircraft, and ships to the Middle East to help defend Saudi Arabia against an Iraqi attack. This massive military buildup received the code name Operation Desert Shield.

In November the United Nations Security Council set a deadline of January 15, 1991, for Iraq to withdraw from Kuwait. (The United Nations Security Council is responsible for maintaining international peace and security. It consists of five permanent member nations—the United States, Russia, Great Britain, France, and China—and ten elected members that serve two-year terms.) Although many world leaders tried to negotiate a peaceful resolution to the crisis, Hussein refused to remove his troops. By the end of 1990, it appeared likely that the coalition allies would have to go to war to force Iraq out of Kuwait. As the march toward war continued, however, some popular opposition emerged in the United States and elsewhere. Protesters held antiwar demonstrations in major cities, and the U.S. Congress held heated debates about whether to give President George H. W. Bush (1924–; served 1989–93) authority to use force against Iraq.

Military buildup in the Persian Gulf

The United States began sending military forces to the Middle East a few days after Iraq invaded Kuwait. American military operations in the region were controlled by U.S. Central Command (CENTCOM), a special branch of the Department of Defense based in Florida. CENTCOM was a unified command, meaning that it could direct all branches of the U.S. military (the U.S. Army, Navy, Air Force, and Marines). The commander in chief of CENTCOM was General H. Norman Schwarzkopf (1934–), who reported directly to General Colin Powell (1937–), chairman of the Joint Chiefs of Staff (the main military advisors to the president, consisting of a chairman and the chief of each branch of the armed services), and Richard Cheney (1941–), the U.S. secretary of defense.

On August 6, 1990, Schwarzkopf and Cheney traveled to Saudi Arabia to establish a formal military alliance. The Saudi leader, King Fahd (1923–; ruled 1982–), agreed to allow American troops to enter his country. Several American warships were already stationed in the Persian Gulf. The U.S. Navy had maintained a presence in the Gulf since the end of World War II (1939–45), and this presence had been expanded during the Iran-Iraq War (1980–88). Its main purposes were to maintain stability in the region and to protect commercial oil tankers. As soon as the agreement with Saudi Arabia was in place, Schwarzkopf began sending American military aircraft and ground forces to the region.

The first U.S. warplanes arrived in the Middle East on August 8. These aircraft included F-15 Eagle fighter planes and E-3 Sentry AWACS (short for Airborne Warning and Control System) radar planes. The first U.S. troops arrived by transport planes on August 9. These forces came from the U.S. Army's 82nd Airborne Division, which always kept a brigade on high alert, ready to be sent to war at a moment's notice.

Over the next few weeks, the American military continued to send troops and equipment to the Middle East in ships and planes. Cargo ships were used to transport heavy gear, such as tanks, helicopters, trucks, and artillery, to the Persian Gulf. On some days, up to 150 ships were on their way to and from Saudi Arabia. If these ships were spaced evenly over the 8,000 miles (12,875 kilometers) between the United States and the Persian Gulf, there would have been a ship every 50 miles (80 kilometers). At one point planes were landing in the Saudi desert every twelve minutes around the clock, carrying troops, weapons, electronic equipment, food, and other supplies. By the end of August, the operations had delivered 72,000 troops and 100,000 tons (90,700 metric tons) of cargo. CENTCOM also moved its headquarters to Riyadh, Saudi Arabia.

The military buildup continued through the fall of 1990. By early November the United States had sent 230,000 troops to the Persian Gulf. On November 8 Bush announced

Members of Congress meet in a strategy session to lend support for a resolution to empower President George H. W. Bush to declare war on Iraq. *AP/Wide World Photos, Inc. Reproduced by permission.*

that he planned to send another 200,000 American soldiers to Saudi Arabia. Operation Desert Shield thus became the largest U.S. military deployment since the Vietnam War (1959–75). About one-third of the U.S. Army and two-thirds of the U.S. Navy and Marines would eventually be stationed in Saudi Arabia and the Persian Gulf.

Other nations contribute

Other nations in the coalition against Iraq sent troops and equipment to the Persian Gulf as well. The states of the Gulf Cooperation Council (Bahrain, Kuwait, Saudi Arabia, Oman, Qatar, and the United Arab Emirates) contributed 145,000 troops, 330 aircraft, and 36 warships to their own defense. (The Gulf Cooperation Council is an organization founded in 1981 to promote peace in the Middle East and avoid outside interference in regional affairs.) Great Britain sent 25,000 troops, 54 aircraft, and 17 warships to help the coalition. Egypt sent 40,000 troops, while Syria added 15,000 more. Denmark, Greece, Norway, Portugal, and Spain each contributed a warship. Russia and several other countries provided two warships each. Japan did not send any military forces, but its government provided financial assistance to the coalition.

By January 1991 more than 500,000 coalition forces were stationed in Saudi Arabia or on ships in the Persian Gulf. They faced roughly 545,000 Iraqi troops in Kuwait and along the border between Iraq and Saudi Arabia. Some people claimed that the coalition's military buildup helped stabilize the situation in the Middle East by forcing Hussein's troops to remain along the border instead of invading Saudi Arabia. But others claimed that the massive buildup showed that Bush and other coalition leaders had already decided to attack Iraq.

Enforcing the UN's economic sanctions

The first mission for the coalition forces in the Persian Gulf was to enforce the economic sanctions against Iraq. A few days after the invasion of Kuwait, the United Nations Security Council had passed Resolution 661, which placed strict restrictions on trade with Iraq. These restrictions (called

an embargo) were intended to punish Hussein for breaking international law by invading Kuwait. Under the sanctions, Iraq was not allowed to sell its oil to other countries, and other countries were not allowed to sell weapons or other goods to Iraq. The embargo applied to everything except humanitarian aid, such as medicine and food needed for the health and welfare of Iraqi civilians (people not involved in the military, including women and children). Many people hoped that the sanctions would hurt the Iraqi economy and make it impossible for Hussein to continue his expensive occupation of Kuwait.

On August 25 the United Nations passed Resolution 665, which gave coalition naval forces the authority to stop and search all ships traveling to and from Iraqi ports in the Persian Gulf. The U.S. Navy stopped the first ship on August 31. During the next six months, coalition forces stopped an average of 40 ships per day and boarded an average of 4 ships per day to search them for illegal cargo. By the start of the

U.S. Defense Secretary Dick Cheney speaks in Riyadh, Saudi Arabia. Chairman of the Joint Chiefs of Staff General Colin Powell (left) and General H. Norman Schwarzkopf (center) are seated in the front row. Photograph by Maury Tannen. AP/Wide World Photos. Reproduced by permission.

Persian Gulf War in January 1991, coalition naval forces had logged a total of 6,960 stops and 832 boardings. Only 36 ships were carrying banned cargo, and these ships were sent to other ports. As quoted in *The Persian Gulf War* by Zachary Kent, General Schwarzkopf noted that the coalition effectively "formed a steel wall around the waters leading to Iraq. Thanks to these superb efforts not one cargo hold, not one crate ... of seaborne contraband [illegal goods] ever touched Saddam Hussein's shores." The trade sanctions were costing the Iraqi economy about $30 million per day.

Moving toward war

As the military buildup continued through the fall of 1990, many world leaders tried to negotiate a peaceful resolution to the crisis. For example, Russia sent high-ranking diplomats to meet with Hussein, and King Hussein (1935–1999; ruled 1953–99) of Jordan (no relation to Saddam Hussein) met frequently with leaders on both sides. As time passed and Iraq continued to occupy Kuwait, however, war began to seem unavoidable.

On November 29 the United Nations Security Council passed Resolution 678, which established a deadline of midnight on January 15, 1991, for Hussein to withdraw his army from Kuwait and comply with all previous UN resolutions. If Iraq continued to occupy Kuwait after the deadline, the Security Council authorized the coalition to use "all necessary means to ... restore international peace and security in the area." Twelve of the fifteen members of the Security Council voted in favor of the resolution, while Yemen and Cuba voted against it and China abstained (did not vote).

The resolution did not convince Hussein to remove his forces from Kuwait. Instead, he responded by making threats against the U.S.-led coalition and Israel. Hussein stated that if his troops were attacked, they would burn Kuwaiti oil wells and create an environmental disaster. He also threatened to use chemical weapons against coalition troops and against Israel. Hussein wanted to draw Israel into the dispute because he knew many of the Arab nations in the coalition had long-standing conflicts with the Jewish state. He believed that the Arab forces would not be willing to fight

alongside Israelis defending their country, and the coalition would fall apart.

Ever since Iraq had invaded Kuwait in August, the Iraqi forces had held hundreds of American and European citizens as hostages. Some of these people had been used as "human shields" to protect key Iraqi military and industrial targets from being attacked by the coalition, for fear of hurting their own people. In early December Hussein announced that he would release all the foreigners being held in Iraq and Kuwait. During the next two weeks the Iraqis released about 565 hostages, including 175 Americans. The U.S. Embassy in Kuwait City was officially closed, and the remaining five diplomats were allowed to leave the country. Some people viewed Hussein's decision to release the foreign hostages as evidence that he was willing to negotiate an end to the crisis. But on December 22 Hussein stated that he had no intention of leaving Kuwait and that his troops planned to use chemical weapons if they were attacked.

Two U.S. Marines crawl toward a barbed-wire fence during an exercise in a Saudi Arabian desert. They are part of a U.S.-led coalition preparing to liberate Iraqi-occupied Kuwait. *©Peter Turnley/Corbis. Reproduced by permission.*

Final efforts to avoid war

As the UN deadline approached, President Bush made one last effort to negotiate a peaceful settlement. On January 9, 1991, U.S. Secretary of State James Baker (1930–) went to Geneva, Switzerland, to meet with Iraqi Foreign Minister Tariq Aziz (1936–). Although Bush made it clear that no deal was possible unless Iraq withdrew from Kuwait, he said that the meeting was "meant to be a firm signal and a broad gesture to show desire for a peaceful resolution to this crisis." Baker and Aziz talked for more than six hours, but the meeting produced no agreement.

During the meeting, Baker gave Aziz a letter from President Bush to Hussein. The letter contained a stern warning about the consequences Iraq would face if it failed to withdraw from Kuwait by the UN deadline. "We stand today at the brink of war between Iraq and the world," it read, according to *Understanding the Crisis in the Persian Gulf* by Peter Cipkowski.

> This is a war that began with your invasion of Kuwait; this is a war that can be ended only by Iraq's full and unconditional compliance with UN Security Council Resolution 678. There can be no reward for aggression. Nor will there be any negotiation. Principle cannot be compromised. However, by its full compliance, Iraq will be able to rejoin the international community.... What is at issue here is not the future of Kuwait—it will be free, its government will be restored—but rather the future of Iraq. This choice is yours to make.... I write this letter not to threaten, but to inform. I do so with no sense of satisfaction, for the people of the United States have no quarrel with the people of Iraq.

After reading the letter, Aziz refused to deliver it to Hussein.

On January 12 the Secretary General of the United Nations, Javier Pérez de Cuellar (1920–), went to Baghdad and met with both Aziz and Hussein. Once again, however, the meeting failed to make any progress toward ending the crisis.

Opposition to war grows

As the Iraqi occupation of Kuwait continued through the fall of 1990, President Bush seemed increasingly determined to go to war against Hussein. In fact,

some observers claimed that Bush had made up his mind to launch an offensive war back in November, when he doubled the number of American troops in the Persian Gulf. The president often made statements that seemed designed to increase support for war among the American people. For example, he described Hussein as an aggressive dictator who could threaten world peace with chemical and nuclear weapons.

But many people in the United States and around the world opposed the massive military buildup in the Persian Gulf. Some people doubted that Hussein, as the leader of a relatively small Arab nation, really posed much of a threat. Others wondered whether freeing Kuwait was worth the cost, estimated at $2 billion per month during Operation Desert Shield, and the potential risk to American soldiers. After all, Kuwait was not a democracy (a form of government in which the people govern the country through elected representatives) before the Iraqi invasion. Most Americans could not

The United Nations Security Council voting on Resolution 661, which placed strict restrictions on trade with Iraq. *AP/Wide World Photos. Reproduced by permission.*

even find the tiny nation on a map. In addition, Iraq did have some historic claims on Kuwaiti territory. Some people argued that the Arab countries of the Middle East should be allowed to settle regional conflicts on their own.

"No blood for oil"

Perhaps the loudest criticism of the military buildup in the Persian Gulf was that the United States was going to war just to protect its supply of oil. At the time the United States imported 50 percent of its oil from foreign countries, and Kuwait and Iraq each controlled about 10 percent of the world's known oil reserves. The U.S. government had a strong interest in preventing Hussein, or anyone else who might be unfriendly to American interests, from controlling too much of the Middle East's oil.

President Bush, whose family had made a fortune in the Texas oil industry, mentioned on several occasions Kuwait's oil supplies as a factor in sending U.S. troops to the Persian Gulf. In a speech before Congress, as quoted in *The March to War* by James Ridgeway, Bush explained that the Gulf region contained the "lion's share" of the world's oil and declared that "we cannot permit a resource so vital to be dominated by one so ruthless [as Hussein]. And we won't." Bush also referred to maintaining the flow of oil from the Persian Gulf as a matter of national security and stated that "our jobs, our way of life" would be at risk if Hussein were allowed to control Kuwait's oil reserves.

Many Americans felt that the nation's dependence on foreign oil was a poor reason to get involved in a costly war. Instead, they argued that the United States should adopt energy policies that would encourage conservation and the development of renewable sources of energy, like solar power, to reduce the nation's dependence on the Middle East. A popular antiwar slogan at the time was "No Blood for Oil!" The Bush administration seemed to recognize that fighting over oil was an unpopular cause. Over time it stopped focusing on protecting Kuwait's oil reserves and emphasized the idea of freeing Kuwait from the Iraqi occupation. The administration argued that the world could not simply stand by while independent nations were overrun by aggressive neighbors.

U.S. Congress debates a declaration of war

Debate over the approaching war took place in homes, schools, and offices across the United States throughout Operation Desert Shield. As the UN deadline neared, the U.S. Congress held a series of heated debates to decide whether to grant President Bush formal permission to use force against Iraq. The president acts as commander in chief of America's armed forces. But the U.S. Constitution gives Congress the sole authority to declare war. The founders of the country wanted to make sure that the people's elected representatives had the final say in whether to enter a war. However, some presidents have used their position as commander in chief to lead the nation's military forces into battle without a formal declaration of war. The Vietnam War (1955–75), for example, was referred to as a "police action," not a war. In trying to persuade Congress to authorize the use of force, Bush said that he was willing to use the American military to force Iraq to leave Kuwait regardless of what Congress decided.

The congressional debates lasted for three days and were broadcast live on television. Many senators and representatives argued that President Bush should wait and give the trade embargo more time to pressure Hussein economically. When the final votes were counted on January 12, however, the Congress had voted to declare war against Iraq if Hussein failed to withdraw from Kuwait by the UN deadline. The resolution passed the U.S. Senate by a vote of 52 to 47 and passed the House of Representatives 250 to 183. It was only the sixth time in the nation's history that Congress had voted to go to war.

Hussein misinterpreted the heated debate in Congress. He believed that the differences of opinion he saw on

A man protesting U.S. involvement in the Persian Gulf War has "No War" painted on the back of his shaved head. ©*Phillip James Corwin/Corbis. Reproduced by permission.*

television meant that the American government was weak and would be torn apart by a war. It was not surprising that he did not understand the concepts of free speech and democratic decision making. After all, Iraqi citizens were not allowed to criticize Hussein or his policies. Hussein bragged that his army would inflict massive casualties (killed and wounded soldiers) on the U.S. forces, and he claimed that American society would never accept the high cost of a war against him.

Contrary to Hussein's beliefs, however, the U.S. government and the American people largely came together as soon as Congress declared war against Iraq. "As soon as the vote was completed, there was a change across the country," recalled Senator Robert Dole (1923–) of Kansas, as quoted in *Understanding the Crisis in the Persian Gulf.* "The people realized that Congress has a role to play, and played it in this situation. The American people were waiting for Congress to make a judgment. When the Congress did, then the people swung behind the president."

Protests continue

However, some people continued to speak out against the coming war, including environmentalists and religious groups like the National Council of Churches. Some Americans held peaceful demonstrations against the war in Washington, D.C., and in other major cities.

Although some people protested President Bush's policies, most Americans still supported the U.S. troops stationed in the Persian Gulf. Throughout Operation Desert Shield, millions of people tied yellow ribbons around trees in their yards to show their hope for the soldiers' safe return. Americans also sent thousands of letters, gifts, and care packages to the troops. The average U.S. soldier in the Gulf received 3.75 pieces of mail per day, including books, candy, and letters of support from complete strangers.

The reaction of the Iraqi people

In the meantime, the people of Iraq were growing increasingly concerned about the possibility of an attack by coalition forces. Many Iraqis supported the invasion of

Experiences of U.S. Soldiers in Operation Desert Shield

The American soldiers who served in Operation Desert Shield were on average twenty-seven years old. Most of them were members of the military reserves, meaning that they were civilians who had received some military training and were called up to serve on active duty when needed. Those who were stationed in Saudi Arabia wore tan uniforms with a desert camouflage pattern. While conducting drills or patrols they also wore bullet-resistant Kevlar helmets and vests. They carried M16 rifles and wore backpacks that held about 60 pounds (27 kilograms) of equipment, including food, water, bedding, and gas masks.

The American ground forces lived in tents in the Saudi desert. Some had difficulty adjusting to the open spaces, the desert heat, and the fine sand that got into their food, weapons, computers, and vehicle engines. The troops usually bathed using a bucket because of the scarce supply of water. They ate mostly prepackaged food called Meals Ready to Eat (MREs). They drove around in sturdy trucks they called Humvees, which was short for High-Mobility Multipurpose Wheeled Vehicles (HMMWV).

The American troops stationed in Saudi Arabia had to adjust to the customs of that country. Saudi life centers on the Islamic religion. People stop whatever they are doing to pray five times a day. Some Muslims objected to King Fahd's decision to allow American military forces—which included Christians, Jews, and women—into Saudi Arabia. In order to minimize conflicts between the American soldiers and their Saudi hosts, General Schwarzkopf issued a special set of rules for the forces in Operation Desert Shield. "Islamic law and Arabic customs prohibit or restrict certain activities which are generally permissible in Western societies," he explained, as quoted in *The Persian Gulf War*.

Out of respect for the Islamic emphasis on modesty, Schwarzkopf's rules banned sexy books and magazines, including bodybuilding publications. The thirty-two thousand American women who served in the Persian Gulf faced a number of limitations on their behavior. They were allowed to drive only on military bases, since Saudi law bans women from driving. They were also required to dress modestly at all times, meaning that they had to keep their arms and legs covered and could not wear bright colors. When men and women went out in public together, they were not allowed to touch each other, and the women were expected to follow the Saudi custom of walking twelve paces behind the men.

Iraqi people in Baghdad burn the U.S. flag as others hold portraits of Iraqi President Saddam Hussein during a demonstration protesting the United States military buildup.
Photograph by Hussein Malla. AP/Wide World Photos. Reproduced by permission.

Kuwait. Others were tired of warfare and opposed Hussein's actions, but they were afraid to speak out because criticizing the government was against the law in Iraq. As the UN deadline approached, many wealthy Iraqis fled the country or left for their summer homes outside Baghdad (Iraq's capital) with the hope of avoiding the future fighting. Other Iraqi citizens gathered at Muslim holy sites in the belief that coalition forces would spare these areas from attack.

Hussein declared January 15, the day of the UN deadline, to be a national "day of challenge." He ordered Iraqi citizens to march through the streets of Baghdad in a show of defiance against the U.S.-led coalition. Hussein even gave students and government workers the day off to ensure a large turnout. About five hundred thousand people showed up at the government-sponsored rallies in downtown Baghdad, where they burned American flags and shouted anti-Bush slogans. But observers noticed that, except for the protesters, the usually busy city of four million people was deserted.

The Air War

The United Nations (UN) deadline of January 15, 1991, passed with no indication that Iraqi President Saddam Hussein (1937–) would withdraw his forces from Kuwait. By this time Iraq had occupied its smaller neighbor for nearly six months. The United States and its allies had sent hundreds of thousands of troops to the Persian Gulf region during this period. Their immediate goal was to prevent Iraqi troops from moving into Saudi Arabia and to enforce economic sanctions (trade restrictions intended to punish a country for breaking international law) against Iraq. This massive military buildup received the code name Operation Desert Shield.

In the early morning hours of January 17, the U.S.-led coalition launched an offensive attack aimed at pushing the Iraqi forces out of Kuwait. Coalition leaders named the offensive Operation Desert Storm. The first phase of the operation involved a series of coordinated air strikes against military targets in Iraq and Kuwait. The idea behind these strikes was to reduce Hussein's military strength and make it impossible to continue his occupation of Kuwait. The air war continued for six weeks and achieved nearly all of the allies' objectives.

The allied attack begins

At around 2:00 AM local time on January 17, eight Apache helicopters from the U.S. Army's 101st Airborne Division left secret air bases in Saudi Arabia and flew across Iraq's western border. They flew close to the ground to avoid being detected by Iraqi radar. They also flew without lights and avoided the remote camps of Arab goat herders so that no one would see or hear them. The Apaches were on an important mission to destroy Iraqi radar stations that provided Hussein's air force with early warnings when enemy aircraft entered the country. The U.S. helicopters managed to knock out two radar stations in a line that stretched across the Iraqi desert, opening a hole in Iraq's radar defenses where coalition aircraft could fly through undetected.

A short time later, hundreds of coalition planes began taking off from air bases in Saudi Arabia and aircraft carriers in the Persian Gulf. The air war had three main goals. The goal of the first wave of air strikes was to destroy Iraq's air-defense capabilities. Toward this end, the coalition attacked Iraqi air bases, destroying many warplanes on the ground and dropping bombs on runways to prevent others from taking off. They also went after Iraq's antiaircraft guns and missiles. Some of the more dangerous targets were hit with cruise missiles and Tomahawk missiles fired from allied warships in the Persian Gulf.

The second wave of allied air strikes was intended to disrupt Iraq's military command and control functions. Some of these targets were located in cities like Baghdad (Iraq's capital) and were surrounded by civilian areas. (Civilians are people who are not involved in fighting a war, including women and children.) American forces used F-117A Stealth fighters—sleek, triangular planes that are almost invisible to radar—equipped with laser-guided "smart" bombs to hit some targets in Baghdad. They knocked out the Iraqi capital's electricity, water, and communication systems in an attempt to paralyze the Iraqi military command. They also destroyed a number of roads and bridges leading to the city.

The goal of the third wave of air strikes was to weaken the Iraqi ground forces in and around Kuwait. The coalition bombed Iraqi defensive positions, destroying hundreds of enemy tanks and other equipment and lowering the

morale of Iraqi troops. The six-week air war eventually involved 2,000 planes from seven countries (the United States, Britain, France, Italy, Canada, Saudi Arabia, and Kuwait). Coalition aircraft flew 110,000 sorties (a sortie is one plane flying one mission) over the course of the war.

A gun is fired aboard the battleship USS *Missouri* as night shelling of Iraqi targets takes place along the northern Kuwaiti coast during Operation Desert Storm. *©Corbis. Reproduced by permission.*

The world watches the war unfold

The first allied air strikes against Baghdad were reported live on television by Western journalists who remained in the Iraqi capital on January 17. The news-gathering network CNN showed footage of the bombing even before the U.S. government officially announced that the war had begun. Some journalists who were staying at the Al Rasheed Hotel in downtown Baghdad told viewers about seeing flashes of light in the sky and hearing explosions. One British reporter stood on his hotel balcony and watched an American missile fly past and smash into the nearby headquarters of the Iraqi air force. This marked the first time in history that the opening strikes of a war were seen live on television.

The official U.S. government announcement regarding the start of the war came at 7:00 PM Eastern time on January 16 (Washington, D.C., is eight hours behind Baghdad). White House spokesman Marlin Fitzwater gave a press briefing in which he stated, "The liberation of Kuwait has begun." Two hours later President George H. W. Bush (1924–; served 1989–93) made a prepared speech on national television. Bush told the American people that negotiations and sanctions had failed to persuade Hussein to withdraw his forces from Kuwait. He then outlined the U.S. strategy of using massive air strikes to destroy Iraq's military capability so that it could no longer threaten its neighbors. Finally, the president stressed: "Our goal is not the conquest of Iraq—it is the liberation of Kuwait."

Iraq fights back with Scud missiles

The day after coalition aircraft and missiles began bombing Baghdad, Hussein followed through on his threat to attack Israel. Israel was created by the United Nations in 1948 as a homeland for all Jewish people. Its location in the Middle East was also the ancient home of an Arab people called the Palestinians, many of whom were displaced by the creation of the Jewish state. This created feelings of resentment and hatred toward Israel throughout the Arab world and led to several bitter wars. Hussein wanted to draw Israel into the war because he thought this might break apart the U.S.-led coalition. The Iraqi leader believed that some Arab nations would leave the coalition or even switch their support to Iraq rather than ally themselves with the Jewish state.

Iraqi forces launched several Scud missiles at targets in Israel on January 18, the day after the air war began. Although the Scud was not a very advanced or accurate missile, it succeeded in frightening the people of Israel. "The Scud was a clumsy, obsolete [out-of-date] Soviet missile, a weapon that could fly 300 miles [480 kilometers] and miss the target by a couple of miles," allied commander General Norman Schwarzkopf (1934–) explained, as quoted in *The Persian Gulf War* by Zachary Kent. "However, the Scud was effective as a

terror weapon against civilian populations." Residents of Israel were concerned that the Iraqi missiles might contain chemical weapons. They carried gas masks everywhere they went and hurried into specially prepared sealed rooms whenever air-raid sirens sounded.

Iraq also launched a Scud missile at a U.S. air base in Dhahran, Saudi Arabia, on the second day of the war. This missile was intercepted and destroyed in midair by an American Patriot missile, marking the first time in history that an attacking missile was destroyed by a defensive missile in combat. The Patriot system used radar to detect and track incoming Scuds, and then programmed course instructions into a defensive missile and launched it. The Patriot missile zeroed in on the Scud and then exploded when it got within range, destroying both missiles.

Following this first success in the skies over Dhahran, the U.S. military installed Patriot missile defense systems in

Sergeant Ken Mahaley, crew chief, launches an F-16C Fighting Falcon Fighter during the first wave of the air attack on Iraq in support of Operation Desert Storm. *Photograph by Staff Sergeant Perry J. Heimer. ©Corbis. Reproduced by permission.*

Israel. This was the first time the United States had acted directly in Israel's defense. Although Israeli leaders made threatening speeches against Iraq, the Israeli government bowed to U.S. political pressure and stayed out of the war, partly because Iraq never used chemical weapons against them. Some experts claimed that Hussein did not possess the technology to deliver deadly chemicals on missiles. Others thought that he probably decided against using chemical weapons against Israel because he was worried that Israel would retaliate with nuclear weapons. (Israel has had atomic bombs since the 1960s.)

Iraq fired a total of eighty-six Scud missiles during the conflict. Forty were aimed at Israel and the rest at Saudi Arabia. The majority of the Scuds were destroyed by Patriot missiles. In Israel, 1 person was killed and 239 wounded by the Iraqi missile attacks on the cities of Tel Aviv and Haifa, while about nine thousand apartments and homes were damaged or destroyed. The deadliest Scud attack hit a U.S. Army Reserve camp in Dhahran, killing twenty-eight American soldiers and wounding eighty more.

An environmental disaster

In addition to launching Scud missiles, Iraqi forces retaliated against the coalition by destroying Kuwaiti oil facilities. On January 22 Iraqi troops began setting Kuwaiti oil wells on fire, creating thick clouds of toxic smoke. On January 25 millions of gallons of oil began spilling into the waters of the Persian Gulf from a terminal used to fill oil tankers. Thick crude oil covered the surface of the gulf with the largest oil slick the world had ever seen, 50 miles (80 kilometers) long and 12 miles (19 kilometers) wide, before the leak was stopped.

Hussein claimed that allied bombing campaigns had caused the oil leak. But coalition leaders accused Iraqi troops of releasing the oil to prevent allied ships from approaching the shore. Some people also believed that the Iraqis released the oil with the hope of damaging the desalinization plants that changed salty seawater into drinking water for Saudi Arabia and other Middle Eastern countries. However, special booms (long floating barriers) were used to contain the spill and prevent it from reaching the desalinization plants. But the oil killed thousands of fish, birds, and marine animals in the Persian Gulf.

Allies achieve air superiority

At the start of the Persian Gulf War, Iraq had the sixth-largest air force in the world. Hussein had 950 planes under his command, located at 54 air bases across the country. To the surprise of many coalition leaders, however, Iraq's air force did not provide organized resistance to the massive allied air assaults. Some of the lack of response was due to the successful allied strikes against Iraqi airports, which destroyed many enemy warplanes on the ground and damaged runways so that others could not take off. But a number of Iraqi pilots chose not to fight the coalition forces and instead flew their planes to neutral Iran. As many as 150 Iraqi aircraft fled to Iran in the early days of the air war, where they were impounded (held) for the rest of the war. Some experts wondered whether this was planned because Hussein had realized that he had little chance of defeating the allies and decided to save some of his planes for use after the war. Of the Iraqi planes that did fight the coalition, 40 were destroyed in air-to-air combat.

As the air war progressed, Iraqi forces shot down a number of coalition planes with their antiaircraft defenses. A total of forty-one coalition aircraft were shot down during the war, thirty-two American planes and nine from other countries. Some of the pilots of these planes were killed. But others parachuted safely to the ground and were either picked up by U.S. search-and-rescue helicopters or captured by Iraqi troops. The American people learned about some of these incidents when Hussein forced the captured airmen to answer questions and make antiwar statements on Iraqi television. Hussein's actions were a direct violation of the Gene-

President George Bush holds a press conference the day after the United States began its attack on Iraq. *Photograph by Doug Mills. AP/Wide World Photos. Reproduced by permission.*

va Conventions (a set of international laws that guarantee the humane treatment of enemy soldiers and prisoners and the protection of civilians during wartime), which outlaw the public display of prisoners of war. President Bush condemned Iraq's mistreatment of its allied prisoners. "If Saddam thinks this brutal treatment of pilots is a way to muster world support, he is dead wrong," Bush said, as quoted in *Understanding the Crisis in the Persian Gulf* by Peter Cipkowski.

On January 23, General Colin Powell (1937–) announced that the coalition forces had achieved air superiority in the Persian Gulf. Powell was the chairman of the Joint Chiefs of Staff (a group of top military advisors to the president of the United States, consisting of a chairman and the chief of each branch of the armed services). His statement meant that the allied air strikes had destroyed all of Iraq's warplanes and antiaircraft guns, so that future air strikes could be launched without any fear of counterattacks from Iraqi forces. By this time, one week into the air war, allied planes had already flown twelve thousand sorties.

Air war takes a toll on Iraq

Once the coalition forces achieved air superiority, they began targeting the Iraqi troops in Kuwait with air strikes. The main goal of these attacks was to weaken the Republican Guard, an elite Iraqi military unit consisting of one hundred thousand men. Republican Guard troops were the best trained, best equipped, and most highly motivated of all of Hussein's forces. Coalition leaders knew that they would eventually face Iraq's Republican Guard in a ground war. "That we will have to take on the Republican Guard in ground-to-ground combat is, in my estimation, guaranteed," said U.S. General Schwarzkopf in *Understanding the Crisis in the Persian Gulf*. The allies used air attacks to "shape the battlefield" in their favor by weakening the Republican Guard before the ground war began.

Over the next few weeks, coalition bombs continuously hit Iraqi defensive positions in Kuwait. These attacks destroyed more than half of Iraq's tanks and artillery in Kuwait. The allies also managed to cut off supplies of food, water, and fuel to the Iraqi forces in Kuwait. Finally, they

dropped millions of leaflets written in Arabic over the Iraqi front lines that urged enemy soldiers to surrender, hoping this would weaken the Iraqis' will to fight.

As the air war continued into February, more people began to express concern about civilian casualties (people who are killed or wounded) and damage to civilian buildings in Iraq. Some critics argued that it was not necessary to destroy Iraq to force Hussein to withdraw from Kuwait. But coalition leaders argued that they needed to destroy resources that could be used to support Iraqi troops in Kuwait. They also claimed that the continued air strikes would help minimize allied casualties once the ground war began.

Iraq offers to withdraw

The first indication that the air war was taking a toll on Hussein's army came on February 15, when Iraq's military leaders announced that they were willing to withdraw from

A residential area lies in ruins after an Iraqi Scud missile attack in Tel Aviv, Israel, on January 18, 1991. *Photographer Martin Cleaver. AP/Wide World Photos. Reproduced by permission.*

Allied fighter-bombers patrol the skies of Iraq during the Persian Gulf War. The coalition air attack took a toll on Iraq's military. ©Stocktrek/Corbis. Reproduced by permission.

Kuwait in accordance with UN resolutions. This was the first time that the Iraqi government had offered to leave Kuwait. Up until this time, Hussein had vowed that he would never give up Kuwait. In fact, according to *Understanding the Crisis in the Persian Gulf,* he once said that it would be "comparable to the United States giving up Hawaii." The offer to withdraw was met with celebration in the streets of Baghdad, a sign that the Iraqi people were growing weary of the war.

However, President Bush rejected the offer because it had unacceptable conditions attached. Hussein offered to leave Kuwait only if Israel withdrew from the Arab territories it had occupied since the Arab-Israeli War of 1967, and if Kuwait formed a new government that did not include the Sabah family, which had ruled the country for many years. Despite this failure of this offer, some world leaders saw it as a positive sign that Iraq was willing to negotiate an end to the war. Mikhail Gorbachev (1931–), president of the Soviet Union, came up with a peace proposal of his own on Febru-

America's Advantage in Weapons Technology

During the Persian Gulf War, the U.S. military introduced a new class of advanced weapons systems that gave the coalition a huge technological advantage over Iraq. These systems increased the effectiveness of traditional weapons and led to vast improvements in the allied military's capabilities.

Much of the coalition's success in the air war could be traced to its ability to locate important targets. The allies used satellites orbiting the Earth to generate data for maps, locate Iraqi military units, and pinpoint locations of air defense and command centers. They also used special planes equipped with powerful radar systems, like AWACS (Airborne Warning and Control System) and JSTARS (Joint Surveillance Target Attack Radar System), to detect and locate aircraft flying over Kuwait as well as tanks and supply vehicles on the ground.

Once the coalition forces located their targets, they used advanced bombs to destroy them. The U.S. Air Force released several videotapes to the media showing laser-guided "smart" bombs hitting targets with pinpoint accuracy. One video showed bombs sailing through the open doors of a bunker where an Iraqi Scud missile was stored. Another showed a bomb going down the rooftop air shaft of the building that served as headquarters for the Iraqi air force. Many of these bombing runs were made at night, with pilots using night-vision goggles to allow them to see their targets. Nighttime bombing runs,—along with electronic jamming to confuse or dis-

able Iraqi radar, helped protect the coalition pilots from antiaircraft fire.

The technologically advanced weapons used by the United States and its allies during the Persian Gulf War helped reduce the number of civilian casualties in Iraq and Kuwait. For example, smart bombs destroyed several military targets in downtown Baghdad while leaving nearby buildings intact. After the first week of the air war, some observers noted, many residents of Baghdad went back to their normal routines, since it was clear that the coalition was only targeting military sites.

Yet the Iraqis did suffer civilian casualties during the air war. The allies made some mistakes in selecting targets, and some bombs missed their intended targets. One of the most controversial attacks took place on February 13, when coalition forces used laser-guided bombs to destroy a bunker in downtown Baghdad, killing one hundred Iraqi women and children who were hiding inside. American officials believed that the bunker was an Iraqi military command center. They pointed out that its roof was painted in camouflage, that it had a barbed-wire fence around it, and that there were computer cables in the wreckage. But Iraqi officials claimed that the bunker was a civilian air-raid shelter. Another controversial attack took place when U.S. planes bombed a factory that was believed to produce chemical weapons. Iraqi officials later presented reporters with evidence that the factory actually produced infant formula.

ary 18, and Iraq agreed to it a few days later. But once again Bush rejected it, saying it did not meet all of the demands of the UN resolutions.

On February 22 Bush set a new deadline of noon on February 23 for the Iraqi troops to withdraw from Kuwait. He warned that the coalition would launch a ground war if Hussein failed to meet the deadline. By this time, coalition planes had flown 94,000 sorties against the Iraqi forces and dropped more than 140,000 tons (127,000 metric tons) of bombs. The air war had achieved its goal of causing severe damage to Iraq's armed forces and their resources. By the end of the war, estimates of the damage to Iraq from allied bombing reached $110 billion, or around $1 million for every allied sortie.

The Ground War | 6

On February 22, 1991, U.S. President George Bush (1924–; served 1989–93) set a deadline of noon the following day for Iraqi President Saddam Hussein (1937–) to withdraw his military forces from neighboring Kuwait. By this time, the U.S.-led coalition had been pounding military targets in Iraq and Kuwait from the air for nearly six weeks. Though the air war had taken a severe toll on the Iraqi forces, Hussein still refused to withdraw. He also promised to cause major damage to the coalition troops if they attacked on the ground.

On February 24 the coalition launched a dramatic ground assault to force the Iraqi troops out of Kuwait. Coalition leaders expected to meet tough resistance from Hussein's army, but they encountered very little. In fact, thousands of desperate Iraqi soldiers surrendered to the advancing coalition forces. The allies achieved a stunning victory in the ground war, successfully liberating Kuwait after only one hundred hours of combat.

The Battle of Khafji

Even though Iraq had suffered terrible damage to its capital city of Baghdad and its military strength during the six weeks of allied air attacks, Hussein remained confident that he could win a ground war. After all, he commanded the fourth-largest army in the world, with nearly one million soldiers. More than half of these soldiers were stationed in and around Kuwait. In addition, Hussein's army was equipped with large quantities of modern Soviet-built weapons and equipment, including four thousand tanks and three thousand long-range artillery (weapons used to launch missiles). Many of his soldiers had had recent combat experience in the Iran-Iraq War (1980–88). Finally, his troops had the advantage of fighting close to their main supply base.

Some historians claim that Hussein actually welcomed a ground war. The Iraqi leader felt that his soldiers were the best defensive fighters in the world. He also thought that the United States and its allies would give up if they started to suffer massive casualties (people killed and wounded in battle). As quoted in *The Persian Gulf War* by Zachary Kent, Hussein warned coalition leaders that his army would engage in "the mother of all battles" and threatened that "whoever collides with Iraq will find columns of dead bodies, which may have a beginning but not an end."

Hussein had tried to prove the strength of his ground forces a few weeks before the coalition launched its ground war. At the end of January he ordered Iraqi troops to make a surprise attack on the town of Khafji, Saudi Arabia. Khafji was a small beachside town located six miles from the Kuwaiti border. The residents of Khafji had abandoned the town two weeks earlier, when the coalition had begun bombing targets in Kuwait. But Khafji still served as a base for a small force of U.S. Marines and Saudi soldiers who were spying on the sixty thousand Iraqi troops in the area.

On January 30 between eight hundred and one thousand Iraqi tanks and armored vehicles rolled into Khafji and took over the town. The allied soldiers managed to hide from the Iraqi invaders for thirty-six hours until help arrived. With the support of U.S. artillery, troops from Saudi Arabia and the nearby Persian Gulf country of Qatar fought an intense day-long battle and reclaimed the town. An American journalist

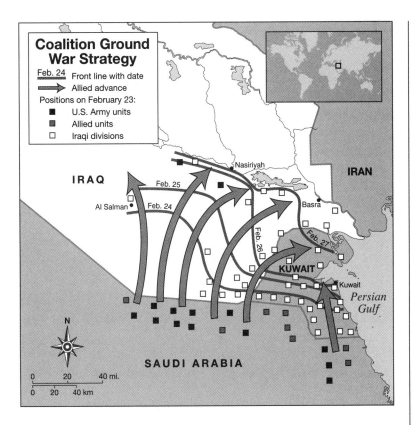

A map of the U.S.-led coalition ground war strategy during the 1991 Persian Gulf War. *Map by XNR Productions, Inc. Thomson Gale. Reproduced by permission.*

who arrived in Khafji a short time later recalled the scene: "Numerous Iraqi, Saudi, and Qatari armored vehicles, some with smoke pouring from the turrets [armored structures that protect mounted guns], lay abandoned in the streets, several still holding the charred bodies of soldiers. Buildings and walls were pockmarked with bullet holes and, in many places, shattered by heavy shells," Chris Hedges wrote in the *New York Times.* "The exhausted Saudi troops, their eyes red after two days of fighting, turned to the few onlookers along the road, raised their weapons over their heads, and shouted 'Allah akhbar!'—God is great!"

The Battle of Khafji was the first ground battle of the Persian Gulf War. Thirty Iraqi soldiers were killed in the fighting, thirty-seven more were wounded, and five hundred were taken prisoner. Eighteen soldiers from the Saudi army were killed and twenty-nine were wounded. Eleven U.S. Marines were also killed during the battle when an American warplane accidentally destroyed their light-armored vehicle. Military experts felt that Hussein had attacked Khafji in order to demonstrate the toughness, discipline, and morale of his army. He may have thought that capturing a town in Saudi Arabia would intimidate coalition leaders and make them reluctant to engage in a ground war. But the commander of the allied forces, U.S. General Norman Schwarzkopf (1934–), was not impressed. According to *Understanding the Crisis in the Persian Gulf* by Peter Cipkowski, he called the Battle of Khafji "as significant as a mosquito on an elephant."

Coalition leaders plan a deception

Though Schwarzkopf downplayed the significance of the Battle of Khafji, it was certainly not the way he and other coalition leaders wanted the ground war to begin. They wanted to wait until the air war had wiped out much of Iraq's military capability. But they knew that an air assault alone would probably not drive the Iraqi forces out of Kuwait. So they eventually planned to launch an all-out attack on the Iraqi army's defensive positions in Kuwait using artillery, tanks, and infantry (foot soldiers). The goal of the ground war was to seize and hold territory in Kuwait until the entire country was under allied control.

Instead of simply attacking the Iraqi defensive positions from the front, however, coalition leaders decided to try to circle around the Iraqi forces in Kuwait and also attack them from the rear. The success of this plan depended on tricking Iraq's military commanders into thinking that the main attack would come from Saudi Arabia (to the south of Kuwait) and the Persian Gulf (east of Kuwait). In the meantime, allied forces planned to secretly move into Iraq (to the west and north of Kuwait). This task was made easier by the fact that the allied air campaign had destroyed Iraq's air defenses, which prevented Iraqi commanders from seeing what was going on around them on the ground.

Coalition leaders came up with a complicated scheme to keep the Iraqi army's attention focused on the south and east. For example, thirty-one allied ships sailed through the Persian Gulf and took positions close to the Kuwaiti coast. These ships carried seventeen thousand amphibious (combined land and sea) forces that made practice landings on the

shore. These maneuvers were intended to convince the Iraqis that the allied assault would come from the Persian Gulf.

A few days before the deadline, Schwarzkopf sent two U.S. Marine task forces with several hundred troops across the Saudi border into Kuwait. Their mission was to clear paths through the Iraqi defenses so that allied tanks and troops could pass through. The Iraqi army had constructed defensive barriers that included rolls of barbed wire, land mines (bombs hidden beneath the ground so that they explode when someone steps on them), walls of sand called berms, and trenches to trap tanks. The Marines broke through these barriers and took up positions a dozen miles into Kuwait. These actions were intended to convince Iraqi commanders that the coalition would attack from the south as soon as the deadline passed.

In the meantime, a large coalition attack force called the VII Corps secretly moved west along the Saudi Arabia–Kuwait border and then north into Iraq. The VII Corps included 250,000

Targeted by Iraqi mortars, U.S. Marines take cover at Khafji, the first ground battle of the Persian Gulf War. *Photograph by Peter De Jong. AP/Wide World Photos. Reproduced by permission.*

allied troops; thousands of tanks and armored vehicles; hundreds of heavy artillery guns; and enough fuel, ammunition, and supplies to last for 60 days of fighting. They moved 500 miles (800 kilometers) without being detected and set up positions that trapped the Iraqi military in Kuwait. "I can't really recall any time in the annals of military history when this number of forces have moved over this distance to put themselves in a position to be able to attack," Schwarzkopf wrote in his book *It Doesn't Take a Hero*. "It was an absolute gigantic accomplishment."

The ground war begins

With the allied forces in place, coalition leaders were ready to launch the ground war if Iraqi troops failed to leave Kuwait by the deadline. The coalition ground forces consisted of 700,000 soldiers from 21 different countries. The majority of these soldiers, approximately 425,000, came from the United States. Saudi Arabia and other Persian Gulf nations contributed 145,000 troops, Egypt added another 40,000, and Great Britain provided 25,000. Many of these soldiers had been stationed in Saudi Arabia for several months and were well trained in desert warfare. The coalition also had more than 100 warships in the Persian Gulf and nearly 2,000 warplanes available for combat missions. They faced roughly 545,000 Iraqi troops that were dug into a series of defensive lines along the Kuwaiti border.

Coalition leaders launched the ground war at 4:00 AM local time on February 24. Back in the United States, where the time difference made it the night of February 23, President Bush announced in a televised speech that "the liberation of Kuwait has now entered a final phase." More than two hundred thousand allied troops swept into Kuwait from Saudi Arabia in the south in the most dramatic armored attack since World War II (1939–45). The columns of tanks encountered little resistance and easily broke through the Iraqi defenses. They reached the outskirts of Kuwait City within twenty-four hours.

The liberation of Kuwait City

As the coalition forces approached Kuwait's capital, the Iraqi defensive lines seemed to fall apart. Iraqi soldiers abandoned their posts and surrendered to the allied troops in waves. Many of these soldiers were desperate for food and

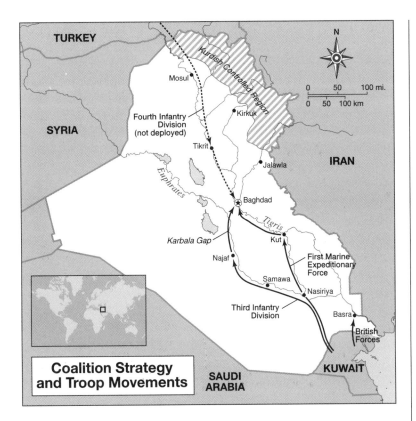

A map showing the coalition strategy and troop movements of U.S. and British forces into Iraq during the Persian Gulf War. *Map by XNR Productions, Inc. Thomson Gale. Reproduced by permission.*

water, and some of them had been wounded in the allied air attacks. Coalition forces ended up taking more than five thousand prisoners in the first ten hours of the battle, and thousands of other Iraqi soldiers surrendered in the next few days.

The desperation of some of the Iraqi troops led to some strange encounters. In one instance, an American pilot was forced to eject from his plane and parachute into the desert. When he landed, dozens of Iraqi troops surrounded him and began trying to surrender to him. In another case, some American soldiers became separated from their unit when their Humvee (short for High-Mobility Multipurpose Wheeled Vehicle) got stuck in the mud. An Iraqi tank pulled their vehicle out and then surrendered to them. The coalition forces had not expected so many Iraqis to surrender and were not prepared to handle it. They had no way of caring for so many prisoners, and mass surrenders slowed the progress of some units.

Despite this unexpected situation, the coalition forces were ready to reclaim Kuwait City by February 27. The

Iraqi troops emerge from a heavily protected bunker to surrender to Saudi soldiers during Operation Desert Storm in southeast Kuwait on February 27, 1991.
Photograph by Laurent Rebours. AP/Wide World Photos. Reproduced by permission.

American troops stepped aside to give Arab forces the glory of liberating the capital. Thousands of happy Kuwaiti citizens rushed to greet the soldiers. "Six months and 25 days after Iraqi tanks crushed Kuwait beneath their treads, another column of armored vehicles rumbled into the capital city," Bruce W. Nelan remembered in *Time*.

> Civilian [people not involved in the war, including women and children] cars formed a convoy around them, horns honking, flags waving. Crowds along the way danced and chanted, 'Allah akhbar!', 'U.S.A.! U.S.A.!', and 'Thank you, thank you!' Thousands swarmed onto the streets, embracing and kissing the arriving soldiers.

In the meantime, the VII Corps continued moving northward across Iraq in an attempt to surround the Iraqi forces in Kuwait. They soon captured Iraq's Al Salman airfield and began using it as a base for coalition air support. While the allies were liberating Kuwait City on February 27, the VII Corps punched through Iraqi defenses to reach the Euphrates River, cutting off the main escape route for

Hussein's troops in Kuwait. The Iraqi occupying forces were trapped.

Many Iraqi units tried to retreat by using the main highway from Kuwait City to the city of Basra in southern Iraq. Some Iraqi soldiers fled in stolen cars and trucks loaded with valuables they had taken from Kuwaiti homes and businesses. But they soon came under attack by coalition tanks, artillery, and air strikes. These attacks turned the road to Basra into a "Highway of Death," creating a 3-mile-long (5-kilometer-long) stretch of road littered with abandoned or burning vehicles. Some allied troops were later criticized for attacking the Iraqi forces while they were attempting to retreat.

Coalition achieves victory in one hundred hours

By the night of February 27, the U.S.-led coalition had taken control of Kuwait as well as 15 percent of Iraq, and

An American Special Forces soldier is mobbed by jubilant Kuwait City residents on February 27, 1991, as the city was liberated from Iraqi forces. *Photograph by Laurent Rebours. AP/Wide World Photos. Reproduced by permission.*

Coalition leaders meet with Iraqi military commanders to discuss an unconditional surrender on March 3, 1991. *Photograph by Sergeant Jose D. Trejo. ©Corbis. Reproduced by permission.*

Hussein's military forces were in full retreat. President Bush appeared on national television to tell the American people that the Persian Gulf War was over. "Kuwait is liberated. Iraq's army is defeated," he stated, as quoted in *A Critical Analysis of the Gulf War* by Colonel Henry G. Summers. "Kuwait is once more in the hands of Kuwaitis in control of their own destiny. We share in their joy, a joy tempered [lessened] only by our compassion for their ordeal." Bush ordered a cease-fire to take effect at midnight Washington time on February 27. "Exactly 100 hours since ground operations commenced [began] and six weeks since the start of Desert Storm, all U.S. and coalition forces will suspend offensive combat operations," he explained.

Hussein ordered his troops to stop fighting the following day. He also sent Iraqi military commanders to meet with coalition leaders to discuss an unconditional surrender. On March 3 Iraq agreed to comply with all United Nations (UN) Security Council resolutions regarding its occupation of

Kuwait. (The Security Council is the division of the United Nations charged with maintaining international peace and security. It consists of five permanent member nations and ten elected members that serve two-year terms.) The following day Iraq began releasing coalition prisoners of war. On March 14 the emir (ruler) of Kuwait returned home and reclaimed control of the government.

The official end of the Persian Gulf War came on April 3, when the Security Council passed Resolution 687. This resolution required both Iraq and Kuwait to respect the border between the two countries and offered UN troops to guarantee the border if necessary. It also required Iraq to destroy or remove all of its biological, chemical, and nuclear weapons and provided for UN inspectors to monitor the process. The resolution held Iraq financially responsible for damages caused by its occupation of Kuwait. It also lifted economic sanctions (trade restrictions intended to punish a country for breaking international law) on shipments of food to Iraq but left all other trade restrictions in place until Iraq disarmed. Iraq agreed to all elements of the resolution on April 6.

General H. Norman Schwarzkopf admitted that he did not expect the U.S.-led coalition's decisive victory over Iraq. *AP/Wide World Photos. Reproduced by permission.*

Iraq suffers a lopsided defeat

In four days of ground combat, coalition forces destroyed an estimated 3,000 Iraqi tanks, or about 75 percent of Hussein's tanks. Thousands of Iraqi soldiers were killed, and about 80,000 were captured by coalition forces. In contrast, the coalition suffered very light casualties, with a total of 240 soldiers killed and 776 wounded during the war. American casualties accounted for 148 of the dead and 458 of the wounded. Some historians claimed that the ratio of Iraqi losses to coalition losses was 1,000 to 1, which made the Persian Gulf War one of the most lopsided in the history of warfare.

The number of casualties among Iraqi civilians was difficult to estimate because Hussein never released that information. Some people said that up to one hundred thousand Iraqi civilians may have been killed or wounded in the war, though military experts later lowered that number to between twenty thousand and thirty-five thousand casualties. Many Iraqis were killed or wounded during allied air strikes against Baghdad. Some bombs missed their targets, while others were intentionally aimed at public highways and other facilities that were used for both military and civilian purposes. Other Iraqi civilians died from a lack of food and water or from the spread of infectious diseases during the war.

The U.S.-led coalition's decisive victory over Iraq in the Persian Gulf War surprised many observers. According to *Understanding the Crisis in the Persian Gulf,* even General Schwarzkopf admitted that "We certainly did not expect it to go this way." Since the end of the war, many people have tried to figure out why the coalition won so easily. Some said it was because the coalition had five months to prepare for the war. Others pointed to the quantity and quality of Saudi air bases, which helped to overcome Iraq's "home-field advantage." Still others gave the credit to superior coalition leadership, well-trained and disciplined U.S. troops, or revolutionary American military technology. Finally, some experts blamed Saddam Hussein for Iraq's terrible defeat, arguing that his overconfidence and strategic errors cost the lives of thousands of his people.

Immediate Aftermath of the War

T he Persian Gulf War ended in a dramatic military victory for the U.S.-led coalition on February 27, 1991. The one-hundred-hour ground war had liberated Kuwait from occupation by Iraq. During the next few weeks, the two sides agreed on the terms of a cease-fire. Iraq ultimately agreed to honor all of the resolutions passed by the United Nations (UN) Security Council. (The Security Council is the division of the UN charged with maintaining international peace and security. It consists of five permanent member nations [the United States, Russia, Great Britain, France, and China] and ten elected members that serve two-year terms.)

Once the war ended, U.S. troops returned home to triumphant celebrations. But some Americans criticized President George H. W. Bush (1924–; served 1989–93) for ending the war while Iraqi leader Saddam Hussein (1937–) was still in power. In the meantime, both Kuwait and Iraq struggled to overcome the terrible destruction the war had caused. Kuwaitis faced the difficult tasks of rebuilding their cities, putting out hundreds of raging oil fires, and moving toward a more democratic society. The Iraqi people rose up in rebellion against

Hussein's weakened government after the war, but Hussein used the remains of his military to crush the uprisings.

U.S. troops return home

Once the Persian Gulf War ended, American troops began returning home at a rate of several thousand per day. The last U.S. troops were withdrawn from southern Iraq by the end of April 1991. They were replaced by a UN peacekeeping force that provided security along the Iraq-Kuwait border.

In the weeks following the war, the American media was full of praise for the troops' strong performance. The returning soldiers were greeted with triumphant celebrations and parades in cities and towns across the United States. President Bush's popularity rose to an all-time high following the successful conclusion of the war.

While the celebrations were continuing, however, some people criticized President Bush's decision to end the war before coalition forces had captured Baghdad. They noted that Hussein remained in power in Iraq, and though the war had reduced his military strength, he still controlled an army of between three hundred thousand and five hundred thousand men. Some critics called the war a "hollow victory" for the United States.

American military leaders admitted that they easily could have pushed on to capture the Iraqi capital and removed Hussein from power. But they pointed out that they had accomplished the main goals of the war: liberating Kuwait from Iraqi control and reducing Hussein's military capability so that he could no longer threaten his neighbors. "We were 150 miles [240 kilometers] away from Baghdad, and there was nobody between us and Baghdad," U.S. General Norman Schwarzkopf (1934–) stated, as quoted in *The Persian Gulf War* by Zachary Kent. "If it had been our intention to take Iraq … we could have done it unopposed…. [But] our intention was purely to eject the Iraqis out of Kuwait and to destroy [Iraq's] military power."

The Bush administration gave several different reasons for ending the war with Hussein still in power. For one, they were worried that the Arab members of the coalition

would not support an American military overthrow of Iraq's government. In addition, they believed that Hussein's position was weak enough that the Iraqi people would rise up and overthrow him on their own. "Saddam Hussein will, in fact, one day be gone," Bush stated, as quoted in *Understanding the Crisis in the Persian Gulf* by Peter Cipkowski. "We can only hope that that day will be soon and that the people of Iraq will have the opportunity to choose a leader who will respect them."

A soldier gives a thumbs up to the crowd during a Desert Storm victory parade in New York. ©*Peter Guttman/Corbis. Reproduced by permission.*

Kuwait works to recover from the war

Although the Persian Gulf War succeeded in freeing Kuwait from Iraqi control, it also left the tiny country struggling to recover from six months of death and destruction. Once the Iraqi forces retreated, most Kuwaiti citizens found themselves without electricity or phone service. Food, water, and medical supplies were hard to find. Unexploded land mines (bombs hidden under the ground so that they explode when someone steps on them) littered the beaches and highways, while the wreckage of Iraqi tanks was scattered across the desert. In addition to the damage caused by coalition bombing campaigns, Kuwait had to repair or replace hundreds of homes and office buildings that had been destroyed or damaged by the Iraqi occupying forces. Some experts thought it would cost at least $50 billion to repair Kuwait's roads, cities, and oil facilities.

The most immediate problem was the damage the fleeing Iraqi troops had done to Kuwait's oil-production facilities. Hussein's forces had set fire to six hundred of Kuwait's one thousand oil wells during the war. They may have done this out of anger and spite, as a way to punish Kuwait for Iraq's defeat, or they may have been trying to make it more difficult for coalition pilots to bomb their targets. In either case, these enormous blazes created thick smoke that made it hard for the coalition troops to see and breathe. The smoke, which was visible for 500 miles (800 kilometers), dimmed sunlight across the Middle East. It also changed regional weather patterns and caused acid rain that damaged farmlands in Iran and India. In fact, black rain and snow were reported as far away as Pakistan and the Soviet Union. Experts feared that if the fires were not put out, they could continue burning for a century.

But the Kuwaiti oil fires were so large and burned so hot that putting them out was very difficult, dangerous, and expensive. Coalition firefighters began examining the damage in mid-March. First the oil fields had to be cleared of land mines before they could begin work. The firefighters laid pipelines to transport tons of seawater to cool the burning wellheads. Then they drilled diagonal "relief wells" to redirect the oil flow and allow them to fill the main wells with cement, putting out the fire. This process of "capping" the burning wells took months and cost up to $10 million per well. The last fire was finally put out in November 1991. By this time, the fires had destroyed roughly ten billion barrels of valuable oil, reducing Kuwait's total oil reserves by 10 to 15 percent.

Iraqi forces created another environmental disaster by releasing millions of barrels of oil from Kuwaiti ports into

American Veterans Suffer from Gulf War Syndrome

Within a year after returning home from service in the Persian Gulf War, thousands of American soldiers developed unexplained health problems. Some of the most common symptoms included headaches, blurred vision, insomnia, short-term memory loss, abdominal pain, diarrhea, skin rashes, and aching joints. The collection of mysterious illnesses suffered by these veterans eventually became known as Gulf War syndrome.

No one knew what had caused the Gulf War veterans to become ill. Some people wondered if they might have been exposed to chemical weapons. These poisonous chemicals could have been used secretly by Iraqi forces or could have been released during coalition bombing of Iraq's chemical weapons plants. Other people thought that the problems might have come from the vaccinations (injections to prevent people from catching certain diseases) and experimental drugs the American forces were given to protect them from chemical and biological warfare. Some people raised the possibility that inhaling smoke from Kuwaiti oil well fires had caused the illnesses. Exposure to some combination of these toxic substances could have damaged the soldiers' nervous and immune systems.

At first the U.S. Department of Defense (DOD) insisted that there was no connection between the veterans' unexplained health problems and their service in the Persian Gulf War. Military officials initially denied that troops had been exposed to chemical or biological weapons during their service in Saudi Arabia, Iraq, and Kuwait. In 1996, however, the U.S. government admitted that up to twenty thousand American soldiers may have been exposed to the toxic nerve gas called sarin during the war.

Later that year the U.S. House of Representatives launched an investigation into the possible causes of Gulf War syndrome. This investigation led to a 1997 report that was highly critical of the DOD and the Veterans Administration. The report claimed that these agencies ignored veterans' complaints and refused to declassify documents that might have helped explain what happened to them. The U.S. Central Intelligence Agency later suggested that the sarin had spread farther than originally thought and may have affected more than one hundred thousand American soldiers.

By the beginning of the twenty-first century more than 110,000 American veterans displayed symptoms of Gulf War syndrome. Hundreds had fallen ill from rare cancers and neurological diseases, and their children were born with birth defects at a rate between two and ten times higher than the national average. Many of these veterans and their families felt abandoned and betrayed by the U.S. government and military, which had long tried to deny that their problems existed. They viewed themselves as the forgotten casualties of the Persian Gulf War.

the waters of the Persian Gulf. The oil spill, which was the largest the world had ever seen, killed thousands of marine birds and animals. It also ruined Saudi Arabia's shrimp industry and threatened the habitat of the endangered dugong (a marine mammal closely related to the manatee). Although special containment booms (long floating barriers) prevented the oil from reaching the desalinization plants (facilities that convert salty seawater into drinking water) along the Saudi coast, it caused a great deal of damage to beaches and shorelines. Experts stated that it would likely take decades for the region's coastal environment to recover.

Kuwait struggles with social problems as well

In addition to the damage to cities, oil facilities, and the environment, Kuwait also struggled to repair its society after the war ended. While most Kuwaitis rejoiced at the liberation of their country, many also lashed out in anger at reminders of the Iraqi occupation. Angry mobs burned the portraits of Saddam Hussein that the Iraqi forces had placed all over Kuwait City. They also tortured and killed at least ten people who were suspected of collaborating with (secretly supporting and helping) the Iraqis, and imprisoned thousands of others.

One target of the Kuwaitis' anger was the country's large Palestinian population. The Palestinians are an Arab people whose ancestors lived in the area of the Middle East that is now covered by the Jewish state of Israel. The creation of Israel in 1948 displaced hundreds of thousands of Palestinians, some of whom eventually settled in Kuwait. Before the Persian Gulf War, Palestinians made up one-third of Kuwait's population. Since the Palestine Liberation Organization (a political group that represents the interests of displaced Palestinians, including reclaiming lost territory from Israel and founding an independent Palestinian state) had supported Iraq during the war, however, many Kuwaitis believed that all Palestinians must have supported Iraq. In 1992 the government of Kuwait forced thousands of Palestinians to leave the country.

Kuwaiti society underwent a number of other changes as a result of the war. The citizens who remained in Kuwait during the Iraqi occupation and the war, and especially those who had joined the resistance movement against

the Iraqis, felt a great deal of bitterness toward the emir and other leaders who fled the country and spent the months of occupation in relative safety. Some members of the resistance openly criticized the emir and demanded a greater say in the government, pointing out that only 10 percent of Kuwait's population had been allowed to vote before the war. The fight for greater democracy (a form of government in which the people direct the country's activities through elected representatives) in Kuwait eventually died down as people focused on the task of rebuilding the country. But in 1992 the emir did follow through on his wartime promise to found an elected parliament that would guide his rule.

A stretch of divided highway leading north out of Kuwait City is lined with damaged military equipment after a coalition bombing. *©Peter Turnley/Corbis. Reproduced by permission.*

Hussein crushes uprisings to remain in power

Iraq also suffered severe damage during the Persian Gulf War. Coalition bombs had destroyed buildings, roads,

Smoke rises from burning oil fields in Kuwait while a military tank waits in the foreground. *©Peter Turnley/Corbis. Reproduced by permission.*

and bridges in Baghdad and other major cities. The country's water, sewer, and electrical systems had been destroyed as well. The total cost of rebuilding Iraq was estimated at more than $100 billion.

The Iraqi people struggled to deal with shortages of food, water, and medical supplies during and after the war. Many survived the war only to fall victim to the epidemics of disease that followed it. There was also some concern that allied bombing of chemical weapons factories and nuclear reactors could have released harmful chemicals or radiation, which could cause long-term damage to people's health.

Iraq's defeat left Hussein's government in a weakened state. Some of his opponents took advantage of the opportunity to try to remove him from power. A few days after the war ended, the Shiite Muslims who lived in the southern part of Iraq launched a major revolt against Hussein's Sunni Muslim government. (Islam is divided into two main branches, Sunni and Shiite. About 90 percent of all Muslims are Sunnis.) The Shiites took to the streets in cities across the south and fought the Iraqi troops that were returning from Kuwait. The rebels took control of many towns, including Basra, and captured the local representatives of Hussein's Baath Party.

But Hussein fought back against the Shiites by using the remains of his powerful army to attack his own people. Iraqi tanks and artillery turned cities into battlefields and killed thousands of civilians in order to crush the uprising. Some reports said that Republican Guard troops fired guns into crowds and bombed civilian neighborhoods with artillery fire. (The Republican Guard was an elite force that was the best-trained and best-equipped part of Iraq's army.) By mid-March Hussein's forces had regained control of Basra.

Kurdish rebellion in the north

In the meantime, the Kurds, a non-Arab Muslim people of northern Iraq, launched another rebellion against Hussein's rule. Hussein's army used force to smash this uprising as well. Iraqi helicopters flew low over Kurdish villages, firing machine guns and dropping bombs. Some Kurds fought back, but many chose to flee the country, fearing that Hussein's forces would use chemical weapons against them, as had happened in 1988. An estimated two million Kurds tried to reach Iran and Turkey in the weeks following the end of the Persian Gulf War. Thousands died along the way of cold and hunger, and thousands more died of disease once they reached the crowded refugee camps. International agencies estimated that one thousand Kurdish refugees died each day in March 1991.

On April 11 President Bush announced a major U.S. relief effort to help the Kurds. American planes

A bombed Iraqi television building. Coalition bombs destroyed many buildings, roads, and bridges in Baghdad and other major Iraqi cities. *©Francoise de Mulder/Corbis. Reproduced by permission.*

dropped packages of food and clothing on the refugee camps during the next several weeks. Eventually the United Nations set up "safe havens" for the Kurds in northern Iraq that were guarded by coalition military forces. Under the terms of the cease-fire agreement that ended the war, the United Nations also created "no-fly zones" over northern and southern Iraq to prevent Hussein from using his air force to attack his political opponents.

Some of the Shiite and Kurdish rebels had believed that they would receive support from the coalition in their efforts to topple Hussein's government. After all, President Bush had made several statements indicating that the U.S. government wanted the Iraqi people to rise up and overthrow Hussein. At one point the U.S. leader encouraged "the Iraqi military and the Iraqi people to take matters into their own hands and force Saddam Hussein, the dictator, to step aside." The rebels interpreted such statements to mean that they would receive American military support.

But the United States and its allies did not provide any direct military assistance to the rebels. Some coalition leaders believed that Iraq might break into three separate countries if the rebels succeeded, adding to the instability of the Persian Gulf region. When the rebellions failed to remove Hussein from power, many Shiite and Kurdish leaders felt betrayed by the coalition. Such feelings became significant twelve years later, when the U.S. government launched a mil-

Kurdish refugees from Iraq living in tents in Turkey in 1991. *©Peter Turnley/Corbis. Reproduced by permission.*

itary invasion of Iraq. Some Iraqis who opposed Hussein still did not trust U.S. leaders and were reluctant to support American troops during the 2003 Iraq War.

Once he crushed the challenges to his rule in 1991, Hussein recalled his elite Republican Guard units to defend Baghdad. He also expelled all foreign journalists from Iraq. Hussein's defeat in the Persian Gulf War had cost him many friends, most of his weapons, and a huge amount of money, but he remained in power. He would continue to defy the world for many years to come.

Inspections and Sanctions, 1992–2000

8

The United Nations (UN) agreement that officially ended the 1991 Persian Gulf War required Iraq to destroy all of its biological, chemical, and nuclear weapons. In the decade after the war ended, however, Iraqi leader Saddam Hussein (1937–) refused to honor the terms of this agreement. He consistently failed to cooperate with the UN weapons inspectors sent to monitor Iraq's progress in destroying its weapons of mass destruction, such as chemical and biological weapons. In fact, he threw the inspectors out of Iraq in 1998. Hussein also made threatening statements toward his neighbors and used military force against his political opponents within Iraq.

Hussein's attitude did not please the United States or other members of the international community. The UN used several different strategies to force Iraq to meet the terms of the 1991 agreement. One strategy involved enforcing economic sanctions (trade restrictions intended to punish a country for breaking international law) against Iraq. Another attempted to limit Hussein's military options by establishing "no-fly zones" over large areas of Iraq. American and British leaders also launched bombing campaigns against Iraq on several occasions in response to Hussein's actions.

United Nations begins weapons inspections

The first international weapons inspections in Iraq took place in May 1991, a month after the Persian Gulf War ended. The International Atomic Energy Agency (IAEA), an organization that promotes the peaceful use of atomic energy, was responsible for inspecting Iraq's nuclear power facilities to ensure that they were not being used for military purposes. The United Nations Special Commission (UNSCOM) was created to oversee the destruction of Iraq's chemical and biological weapons programs and long-range missile projects. The Iraqi government at first agreed to grant the inspectors unlimited access to all of its facilities. But it soon became clear that Iraq was determined to hide the full extent of its weapons programs.

Immediately after the 1991 Persian Gulf War ended, the U.S.-led coalition created a "no-fly zone" in southern Iraq. They declared this area off-limits to Iraqi military aircraft in order to prevent Hussein's Sunni Muslim government from attacking its Shiite Muslim opponents, who were largely located in the south. (Islam is divided into two main branches, Sunni and Shiite. About 90 percent of all Muslims are Sunnis.) American and British aircraft patrolled this area constantly. They occasionally encountered Iraqi planes that were attempting to enter the no-fly zone. U.S. leaders also created a second no-fly zone in northern Iraq to protect the Kurdish people from attack by Hussein's military. (The Kurds are a non-Arab Muslim people of northern Iraq.) Together, the two zones covered a total of 104,600 square miles (270,900 square kilometers), or about 62 percent of Iraq.

Hussein claimed that the United States had created the zones illegally, without the authority of a UN resolution. He also argued that the zones violated Iraq's rights as an independent nation. But U.S. leaders said that the zones were necessary to "contain" Hussein and prevent him from harassing his political opponents. "The no-fly zones have been and will remain an important part of our containment policy," U.S. President Bill Clinton (1946–; served

A Gulf War Veteran Questions the Decision to Leave Saddam Hussein in Power

Some Americans questioned President George H. W. Bush's decision to end the 1991 Persian Gulf War while Iraqi leader Saddam Hussein was still in power. After all, Hussein was known as a brutal dictator who used violence and even chemical weapons to silence his political opponents. Although Hussein suffered a terrible defeat in the war, he still boasted a large army.

Sergeant Dan Welch, who fought in the Persian Gulf War as a tank commander with the VII Corps, wrote a letter to his mother back in Maine a week after the fighting ended. In this letter, Welch worries that the U.S.-led coalition did not go far enough in fighting the war. He says that he wished coalition forces had captured Baghdad, or at least provided assistance to the Iraqi rebels who were struggling to overthrow Hussein's government. Welch feels sorry for the Iraqi soldiers he fought against, some of whom were forced to fight and suffered severe shortages of food and water during the six-week conflict. He ends his letter by wondering whether American troops would someday have to return to Iraq to finish the job they started.

I think we've made a mistake and not finished this the way it should have ended. There is now a weakness in my heart for the people of Iraq. I'm still trying to explain what has gone on here....

It may appear to most of us over here and to you back home that we've done our jobs, but we've screwed up and didn't finish it. [Saddam Hussein is] still alive, and unless somehow the rebels finish what we've started, we may be back....

But I still think we did the right thing, although we didn't go far enough.

Hussein held on to power after the 1991 war by using the remains of his army to crush a series of rebellions by Iraqi citizens. Over the next decade, he continued to threaten his neighbors and refused to honor the terms of the United Nations (UN) agreement that had officially ended the war. For example, Hussein consistently failed to cooperate with UN weapons inspectors who were sent to monitor Iraq's progress in destroying its biological, chemical, and nuclear weapons. Just as Sergeant Welch predicted, in 2003 the United States entered another war to disarm Iraq and remove Hussein from power.

Source: Carroll, Andrew, ed. War Letters: Extraordinary Correspondence from American Wars. New York: Scribner, 2001.

1993–2001) explained, as quoted by *Online NewsHour*. "Because we effectively control the skies over much of Iraq, Saddam has been unable to use air power to repress [control through use of force] his own people or to lash out again at his neighbors." The United Nations never formally recognized the no-fly zones, and they remained the subject of controversy throughout the 1990s.

Clinton defeated George H. W. Bush (1924–; served 1989–93) in the November 1992 American presidential election and took office in January 1993. Hussein viewed the months between Clinton's election and inauguration (a formal ceremony for taking office) as an opportunity to challenge the restrictions that had been placed on Iraq after the Persian Gulf War. Iraq's level of cooperation with the UN inspectors began to decrease during this time. Hussein also ignored warnings to remove anti-aircraft missiles from the southern no-fly zone. In January 1993 the U.S.-led coalition responded by launching a bombing campaign to destroy suspected Iraqi weapons facilities. One U.S. cruise missile missed its target in Baghdad and hit the Al Rasheed Hotel, killing three civilians (people not involved in a military conflict, including women and children).

Iraq plots to assassinate President Bush

Another confrontation erupted between the United States and Iraq just a few months later. In April 1993 former president George Bush accepted an official invitation to visit Kuwait. A few days before Bush's scheduled arrival, Kuwaiti security forces uncovered a plot to assassinate the former U.S. leader. American and Kuwaiti authorities conducted an investigation, which produced evidence linking the plot to Iraq. They claimed that Hussein had ordered the Iraqi Intelligence Service (IIS) to murder his Persian Gulf War rival while Bush was in the Middle East.

On June 27 the U.S. military launched twenty-four Tomahawk missiles from warships in the Persian Gulf and the Red Sea (a long, narrow sea that stretches along Saudi Arabia's western border). The missiles completely destroyed the IIS headquarters in Baghdad. "The Iraqi attack against President Bush was an attack against our country, and against all Americans," President Clinton noted. "We could not, and have not, let such action against our nation go unanswered." Unfortunately, three missiles missed their targets and struck neighboring buildings. Eight civilians were killed, including a leading Iraqi artist, Leila Attar.

In October 1994 Hussein once again threatened to invade Kuwait. He moved Iraq's military forces to the Kuwaiti border, but he withdrew when the United States sent a group of aircraft carriers and fifty-four thousand troops into the Persian Gulf.

An U.S. Falcon 16 CJ plane patrols the no-fly zones established after the 1991 Gulf War. *Photograph by Mike Stewart. ©Corbis Sygma. Reproduced by permission.*

Economic sanctions create hardships for the Iraqi people

As part of the agreement that ended the 1991 war, the UN continued to enforce economic sanctions against Iraq.

These trade restrictions prevented Iraq from selling oil in world markets or buying many types of goods from other countries. The sanctions were originally intended to prevent Hussein from rebuilding his military after the war. Over time, however, the sanctions created severe hardships for the Iraqi people.

Before the 1991 Persian Gulf War, the Iraqi government used the money from its oil sales to buy food from other countries. In fact, Iraq imported 70 percent of its food during the 1980s (less than 15 percent of Iraq's land can be used to grow food). But the postwar ban on oil sales left Iraq with limited funds to buy food. Even worse, the UN economic sanctions banned Iraq from importing fertilizers and pesticides because they could potentially be used to make bombs. Without these materials, Iraqi farmers found it difficult to increase their crop production to make up for the loss of imported food. Instead, Iraq was forced to depend on humanitarian aid to feed its people. But the shipments of food that arrived from the UN and international relief organizations only provided 1,300 calories per day for each Iraqi citizen, which was barely enough to keep an average person alive. The shortage of food led to widespread malnutrition (a physical condition resulting from a lack of adequate food). A UN study released in early 1998 found that severe malnutrition affected 30 percent of Iraq's population.

The people of Iraq also suffered from extreme shortages of safe drinking water. Iraq has always drawn its water from the Tigris and Euphrates Rivers. Before the war this water passed through chemical treatment plants to make it safe for drinking. Likewise, sewage passed through waste treatment facilities to kill harmful bacteria before it was released back into the rivers. But many of these plants were destroyed during the war, and others suffered afterward from a lack of maintenance. The UN economic sanctions prevented Iraq from obtaining many of the chemicals and pumps needed to keep the treatment facilities working. The lack of safe drinking water led to a sharp rise in the number of people suffering from waterborne diseases, such as cholera, typhoid, and dysentery.

Over time, the UN economic sanctions significantly changed the structure of Iraqi society. Before the 1991 Persian Gulf War, Iraq boasted a substantial middle class and a 90 percent literacy rate. But the shortages of basic goods after the war

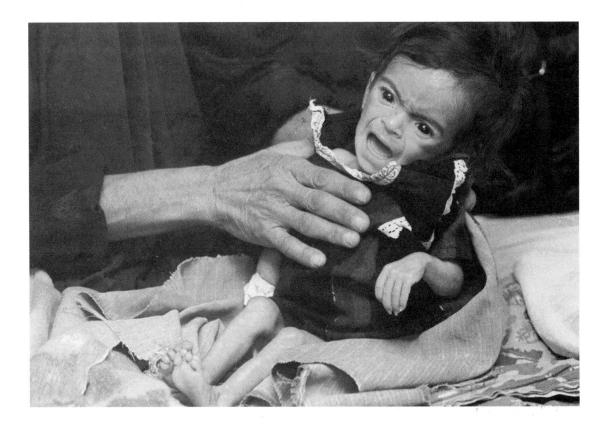

caused prices to rise rapidly. As Thomas E. White noted in *Reconstructing Eden,* by 1995 the price of basic goods increased to 850 times the level found in 1990. This meant that an item that cost $1 in 1990 would have cost $850 in 1995. The salaries of middle-class workers failed to keep pace with the rising prices, so people were able to buy less and less with their paychecks. According to Dilip Hiro in *Neighbors, Not Friends,* a senior civil servant in Iraq earned the equivalent of U.S. $960 per month before the war. Afterward this salary was worth only about $5 due to inflation. As a result, average people could no longer afford to buy even basic necessities. As Iraq's middle class descended into poverty, 25 percent of Iraqi children left school to work to help support their families. The only people who lived well under the sanctions were smugglers and high-ranking officials in Hussein's government.

In 1995 the United Nations began to address the hardships suffered by the Iraqi people under four years of economic sanctions. That April the UN Security Council

A malnourished child is comforted by her grandmother at a Hospital in Baghdad. Due to economic sanctions, 30 percent of Iraq's population suffered from by malnutrition. *Photograph by Peter De Jong. AP/Wide World Photos. Reproduced by permission.*

passed Resolution 986, which allowed Iraq to sell limited amounts of oil in order to buy food for its people. (The Security Council is the division of the United Nations charged with maintaining international peace and security. It consists of five permanent member nations—the United States, Russia, Great Britain, France, and China—and ten elected members that serve two-year terms.) When the "oil for food" program went into effect in December 1996, it marked the first time Iraq had sold its oil internationally since 1990. But the program provided only limited relief for the Iraqi people, increasing the average citizen's food intake to 2,000 calories per day. The United Nations set aside 25 percent of the proceeds from Iraq's oil sales to help Kuwait recover from damages caused by the Iraqi invasion. In addition to food, the remaining income from this program had to cover medicine, approved fertilizers, chemicals for sewage treatment, and spare parts for water pumps.

International community questions sanctions

In 1999 the United Nations Children's Fund (UNICEF), an organization focused on improving children's lives worldwide, released a study evaluating the effects of the economic sanctions on the Iraqi people. The researchers reported that the sanctions had contributed to the deaths of five hundred thousand Iraqi children, or an average of five thousand per month, between 1991 and 1998. UNICEF also estimated that an additional five hundred thousand Iraqi adults had died as a result of the sanctions during this time. Several independent studies produced similar results. The leading causes of deaths that could have been prevented by lifting the sanctions included malnutrition, waterborne illnesses, and untreated medical conditions.

Many members of the international community were horrified by such statistics. They were outraged that the Iraqi people were forced to suffer for Hussein's aggression. One leading figure who spoke out against the sanctions was Pope John Paul II (1920–). In a January 1998 address, quoted by Patrick and Andrew Cockburn in *The Saddam Hussein Reader,* the Pope declared:

> We cry out in anguish over seven years of United Nations sanctions against the Iraqi people, which can only be under-

stood as biological warfare against a civilian population. During the Gulf War, U.S.-led coalition forces deliberately [purposely] targeted Iraq's infrastructure, destroying its ability to provide food, water, and sanitation to its civilian population and unleashing disease and starvation on an unimaginable scale.... We are ashamed that the actions of the United Nations, whose mission is to foster peace, can be so deliberately directed toward the sustained slaughter of innocent civilians.

The assistant secretary-general of the United Nations, Denis Halliday, resigned in 1998 after thirty-five years of service in protest against the continued sanctions. "The policy of economic sanctions is totally bankrupt. We are in the process of destroying an entire society. It is as simple as that," he stated, as quoted by John Pilger in *The Saddam Hussein Reader.* The policy "satisfies the definition of genocide: a deliberate policy that has effectively killed well over a million individuals, children and adults," Halliday continued. "We all know that the regime, Saddam Hussein, is not paying the price for economic sanctions. On the contrary, he has been strengthened by them."

In fact, the sanctions did seem to help support Hussein's rule in some ways. The suffering of ordinary Iraqi citizens created anger throughout the Middle East and created rifts in the coalition that had supported the United States during the 1991 war. As public sympathy toward Iraq increased, various countries in the Arab world began to mend their differences with Hussein. "Iraqi President Saddam Hussein is only a human being who has made mistakes," said United Arab Emirates President Zaid al Nahyan, as quoted in *Neighbors, Not Friends.* "It is time to lift sanctions because it is the Iraqi people who are paying for his mistakes.

The United States insists on continuing sanctions

As the sanctions continued into the late 1990s, several members of the UN Security Council expressed doubts about their effectiveness. France and Russia proposed setting specific conditions for Iraq's disarmament that would end the sanctions once those conditions were met. But the United States refused to consider lifting the sanctions. Officials in the Clinton administration insisted that the sanctions were a vital part of the United Nations's efforts to limit Hussein's power and prevent Iraq from posing a threat to world peace. They denied that the sanctions were responsible for the suffering of the Iraqi people, claiming that UN relief efforts provided more than enough food and money. The administration pointed to evidence showing that Hussein was diverting the humanitarian aid to enrich himself and build up his military.

The Clinton administration's determination to continue the sanctions against Iraq caused controversy in the United States as well. In February 2000, 70 members of the U.S. House of Representatives signed a letter asking President Clinton to lift the economic sanctions against Iraq. But 125 other representatives signed a letter expressing their support for continued sanctions. "The UN oil-for-food program has given Saddam Hussein the opportunity to provide basic needs to his people, but he has squandered [wasted] huge sums of money on arms and luxury goods," Democratic Representative Nita Lowey (1937–) of New York, who signed the second letter, told *The Progressive*. "I am horrified by the images of Iraqis who do not have enough food and shelter, but this is a product of tyrannical [harsh or brutal] leadership, not UN sanctions. Lifting sanctions will only bolster Saddam Hussein's coffers [treasury] and enable him to buy weapons of mass destruction. It will not help the Iraqi people."

Clinton administration officials insisted that the sanctions should remain in place until Hussein was removed from power or the UN saw significant changes in the "policies and practices" of the Iraqi government. But this sometimes made the administration seem indifferent to the suffering of the Iraqi people. Secretary of State Madeleine Albright (1937–) seemed to confirm this charge in a 1996 interview for the television show "60 Minutes." As quoted in *Neighbors, Not Friends,* interviewer Lesley Stahl (1941–) asked, "More than 500,000 Iraqi children are already dead as a direct result of the UN sanctions. Do you think the price is worth paying?" Albright replied, "It is a difficult question. But, yes, we think the price is worth it." In February 1998, when Albright discussed the Clinton administration's Iraq policy at Ohio State University, she was heckled by angry U.S. citizens. This event was broadcast live around the world on the Cable News Network (CNN) and embarrassed the Clinton administration.

For his part, Hussein claimed that Iraq had met the conditions of the UN Security Council resolutions that had ended the 1991 Persian Gulf War and argued that the sanctions should be lifted immediately. "Iraq has complied with and implemented all the relevant resolutions," he stated, as quoted by Patrick and Andrew Cockburn in *The Saddam Hussein Reader.* "There is absolutely nothing else. We demand with unequivocal [unmistakable] clarity that the Security Council fulfill its commitments toward Iraq…. The practical expression of this is to respect Iraq's sovereignty [independence] and totally lift the blockade [economic sanctions] imposed on Iraq."

Iraq's postwar problems continue

Throughout this period, Iraq continued to suffer from internal turmoil. Both of its large minority groups, the Shiites of southern Iraq and the Kurds of northern Iraq, periodically rose up in opposition to Hussein's rule. But Hussein violently suppressed all opposition. In 1995, for example, two of his sons-in-law fled to Jordan. They hoped to serve as leaders in a U.S.-backed opposition government that would replace Hussein. They returned to Iraq six months later, after Hussein promised to forgive them, but were executed shortly after their return.

In August 1996 Hussein once again used force against the Kurds. In response to an armed conflict between two groups of Kurds, he sent troops into the independent Kurdish region of northern Iraq. The troops easily captured Irbil, the capital city of the Kurdish region. Turkey and Jordan were so impressed by Iraq's show of military strength that they stopped cooperating with U.S. efforts to overthrow Hussein's government. U.S. and British forces responded to the capture of Irbil by expanding the no-fly zone in northern Iraq and bombing a number of military targets.

In December 1996 Hussein's eldest son, Uday Hussein (1964–2003), was seriously wounded in an assassination at-

Secretary of State Madeleine Albright was a firm supporter of the Clinton administration's policy of continuing economic sanctions against Iraq. *Photograph by Rick Wilking. Getty Images. Reproduced by permission.*

In this 1998 photo UN weapons inspectors find Iraqi rockets filled with the chemical nerve agent sarin, which were reportedly destroyed by Iraq after the 1991 Gulf War. *AP/Wide World Photos. Reproduced by permission.*

tempt by members of a Shiite resistance group. Gunmen attacked his car as he traveled through an upscale neighborhood of Baghdad, killing his driver and bodyguard. Uday was hit by eight bullets, including one that lodged in his spine. He spent six months in the hospital recovering from his injuries.

Hussein responded to the attack on his son by increasing his efforts to destroy all opposition to his rule. He used violence, including torture and execution, to control or do away with his political enemies. In 1999 the UN Commission on Human Rights condemned Hussein for "the systematic, widespread, and extremely grave violations of human rights and of international law by the Government of Iraq."

Weapons inspectors leave Iraq

In the meantime, Hussein continued interfering with the work of UN weapons inspectors. He consistently refused to allow the inspectors access to certain areas. He also placed restrictions on the inspectors' activities, like forcing them to travel in the company of Iraqi security personnel. In November 1997 Hussein expelled the UN inspectors from Iraq, but Russian diplomat Yevgeny Primakov (1929–) helped negotiate their quick return. In January 1998 Hussein blocked another UN inspection team from entering the country because he felt that it included too many American and British members. He claimed that these inspectors were acting as spies for their governments.

In October 1998 Iraq ended all cooperation with the UN weapons inspections. The United States and Great Britain warned that they would attack Iraq if Hussein refused to allow the inspectors to complete their work. The UN negotiated an agreement that allowed the inspectors to return to Iraq the following month. But Iraqi officials still denied the inspectors access to Hussein's palaces, security offices, and other "presidential sites." The inspectors withdrew within a month, saying that Iraq's lack of cooperation made it impossible for them to do their jobs.

U.S. President Bill Clinton addresses the American people about Operation Desert Fox, the new campaign against Iraq. *Photograph by Richard Ellis. ©Corbis Sygma. Reproduced by permission.*

Operation Desert Fox

At this point American and British military forces launched Operation Desert Fox, a massive bombing campaign aimed at destroying sites that were suspected to have weapons of mass destruction. The attacks began on December 16, 1998, and lasted for three days. During this time the U.S. and British forces fired four hundred cruise missiles and dropped six hundred laser-guided bombs on targets in Iraq.

The renewed bombing of Iraq met with severe criticism from much of the world. The Arab League officially condemned the attacks, and protests broke out across the Middle

East. (The Arab League is an alliance of about twenty Arab nations and the Palestine Liberation Organization that promotes political, military, and economic cooperation in the Arab world.) Several members of the UN Security Council argued that President Clinton had ordered the bombing without the authority of a UN resolution. Russia withdrew its ambassador from the United States in protest.

Within the United States, some critics claimed that President Clinton had ordered the attack to distract public attention from other problems affecting his presidency. The bombing of Iraq began one day before the U.S. House of Representatives was scheduled to begin impeachment hearings against Clinton. The U.S. Constitution says that all federal officials can be impeached, or brought up on legal charges, and removed from elected office if they are found guilty of a crime. The House of Representatives brings the charges and acts as prosecutor, while the Senate hears the case and votes as a jury. The House delayed the impeachment hearings for only one day due to the military action in Iraq. On December 19, members voted to impeach Clinton on charges that he lied to investigators about his affair with a White House intern named Monica Lewinsky (1973–). A few hours later, the president stopped the bombing of Iraq.

In 1999 the UN Security Council passed a new resolution regarding Iraq. Resolution 1284 established the UN Monitoring, Verification, and Inspection Commission (UNMOVIC) to replace UNSCOM. The Security Council hoped that UNMOVIC inspectors would be more acceptable to Iraq and less likely to be accused of spying, since they did not represent individual countries. The resolution also removed all limits on Iraq's sale of oil to other countries, thus making more funds available to buy food and medicine for the Iraqi people. Finally, it provided for economic sanctions to be lifted if Iraq cooperated fully with UNMOVIC inspectors.

Confrontations continued in the no-fly zones throughout 1999 and 2000. In fact, Hussein offered rewards to members of the Iraqi military for shooting down American planes. Nevertheless, the international community made little effort to enforce the UN agreement that had ended the 1991 war. As a result, Iraq was free to operate its weapons programs largely without monitoring for the next four years.

U.S. Policy Moves toward Regime Change in Iraq, 2001–02

9

George W. Bush (1946–), son of the former president who had held office during the 1991 Persian Gulf War, became president of the United States in January 2001. Bush vowed to follow a tougher policy toward Iraq than had the previous president, Bill Clinton (1946–; served 1993–2001). Following the terrorist attacks against the United States on September 11, 2001, the Bush administration launched a global "war against terrorism." In January 2002 Bush expanded the focus of this war to include countries that he believed supported terrorism, including Iraq.

Over the next year Bush pushed for "regime change" in Iraq, a term he used to mean removing Saddam Hussein (1937–) from power. He challenged the United Nations (UN) to enforce the agreement that had ended the 1991 Persian Gulf War, which required Iraq to destroy all of its biological, chemical, and nuclear weapons. In November 2002 the UN Security Council passed Resolution 1441, which authorized a new round of weapons inspections and warned that Iraq would face "serious consequences" if it failed to cooperate. (The Security Council is the division of the United Nations charged with maintaining international peace and security. It consists of five permanent member nations—the United States, Russia, Great Britain, France, and China—and ten elected members that serve two-year terms.) Although Iraq allowed the weapons inspectors to return, Bush continued to argue that Iraq posed a significant threat to world security. He claimed that Hussein still possessed weapons of mass destruction and could supply such weapons to terrorists. Despite a lack of UN support, the United States launched another war against Iraq in March 2003.

Bush launches the war against terrorism

George W. Bush took office as president of the United States in January 2001. During his presidential campaign, Bush had promised to take a tougher position toward Iraq. "I'm just as frustrated as many Americans are that Saddam Hussein still lives," the candidate told journalist Jim Lehrer (1934–) of the TV program "NewsHour" in February 2000. "I will tell you this: If we catch him developing weapons of mass destruction in any way, shape, or form, I'll deal with that in a way that he won't like." Bush followed through on his promise once he was elected. His first military order, issued in February 2001, approved air strikes against targets located near the capital city of Baghdad, outside the "no-fly zones." He said the strikes were intended to warn Hussein that he must respect the zones. (The no-fly zones were set up after the 1991 Persian Gulf War. They covered the northern and southern regions of Iraq, and were intended to prevent Hussein from using military force against his political opponents in those regions.)

Later that year, a national tragedy dramatically changed U.S. attitudes toward unfriendly governments. On September 11, 2001, radical Islamic terrorists hijacked four commercial airplanes. Two of the planes were crashed into the World Trade Center towers in New York City and a third plane was flown into the Pentagon building in Washington, D.C. The fourth hijacked plane crashed into a Pennsylvania field before reaching its intended target. The attacks claimed nearly three thousand lives. U.S. government officials soon traced the plot back to a radical Islamic organization called Al Qaeda, which was led by a Muslim cleric (religious leader)

Iraqi officials present the entire 11,807-page Iraqi declaration of weapons of mass destruction programs. The materials were presented one day before a UN Security Council deadline. *Photograph by Scott Peterson. Getty Images. Reproduced by permission.*

named Osama bin Laden (1957–). (The phrase *al qaeda* means "the base" or "foundation.") Bin Laden hated what he viewed as growing American influence over the Arab world. He formed Al Qaeda in part because he resented the stationing of U.S. troops in Saudi Arabia during and after the 1991 Persian Gulf War. Saudi Arabia is home to the sacred Muslim sites of Mecca and Medina, where millions of Islamic pilgrims travel every year. Like many other Muslims around the world, bin Laden felt that the presence of foreign troops in the Islamic holy land was deeply offensive to his religious beliefs.

In the wake of the September 11 attacks, the Bush administration placed a new emphasis on national security. It announced a "war against terrorism" that at first focused on Al Qaeda and other known terrorist groups. U.S. intelligence experts quickly tracked bin Laden to Afghanistan, a country located east of Iran and north of Pakistan, on the edge of the Middle East. Afghanistan is one of the poorest countries in the world, and it has struggled with political instability and violence for many years. In 1996 a radical Islamic group called the Taliban took over the government and forced strict laws on the Afghan people. Among other things, these laws banned women from working or attending school and required them to wear a tentlike covering called a *burqa* whenever they went out in public. Some Afghan women were stoned to death for disobeying the Taliban's laws.

The U.S. government demanded that the Taliban turn over bin Laden and other members of Al Qaeda so that they could be tried for organizing the September 11 attacks. But the Taliban saw bin Laden as a hero to the fundamentalist Islamic cause and refused. In October 2001 the U.S. military launched Operation Enduring Freedom, a series of air strikes that targeted Taliban military capabilities and Al Qaeda training facilities in Afghanistan. The U.S. also provided military support to the Northern Alliance, an Afghan opposition group that had long fought the Taliban. Although the U.S. troops and their Afghan allies soon removed the Taliban from power, bin Laden escaped. Still, Bush administration officials claimed that they had won their first victory in their war against terrorism by destroying the home base of Al Qaeda.

The "axis of evil"

In early 2002 Bush announced a second phase in the war on terror. He officially expanded the fight against terrorism to include nations that sheltered terrorists or provided weapons, training, or financial support for their activities. Among the countries that he accused of supporting terrorists were Iraq, Iran, and North Korea.

In his first State of the Union address, delivered on January 29, 2002, Bush labeled these three countries an "axis of evil." Although there was no clear link between these governments and Al Qaeda, Bush claimed that they posed a threat to world security because they could provide terrorists with weapons of mass destruction. "The Iraqi regime has plotted to develop anthrax [a deadly bacteria], and nerve gas, and nuclear weapons for over a decade," Bush stated, as quoted by *Online NewsHour.* "This is a regime that agreed to international inspections, then kicked out

A hijacked airplane prepares to crash into the south tower of the World Trade Center in New York on September 11, 2001. After these attacks, the Bush administration announced a "war against terrorism." *Photograph by Carmen Taylor. AP/Wide World Photos. Reproduced by permission.*

the inspectors. This is a regime that has something to hide from the civilized world. States like [Iraq, Iran, and North Korea], and their terrorist allies, constitute an axis of evil, arming to threaten the peace of the world." The phrase "axis of evil" was highly controversial, in part because it suggested an alliance between the three nations that did not exist, and in part because it reminded people of the Axis powers of World War II (1939–45)—Italy, Germany, and

Japan—that had caused so much destruction and death a half-century before.

Over the next few months, officials in the Bush administration began talking about the importance of "regime change" in Iraq. For example, in April 2002 Secretary of State Colin Powell (1937–) told a Senate committee that Iraq "remains a significant threat to the region's stability," and added that "we believe strongly in regime change in Iraq."

Bush challenges the United Nations to take action

In September 2002 Bush challenged the UN to take action against Iraq. He argued that the UN should force Iraq to honor the agreement that had ended the Persian Gulf War eleven years earlier. He claimed that the UN would lose its ability to enforce world peace if it allowed Hussein to continue ignoring the agreement. "Iraq has answered a decade of UN demands with a decade of defiance," he said, as quoted in *A Time of Our Choosing* by Todd Purdum. "All the world now faces a test and the United Nations a difficult and defining moment. Are Security Council resolutions to be honored and enforced, or cast aside without consequence? Will the United Nations serve the purpose of its founding, or will it be irrelevant?" Bush also made it clear that the United States would act alone to disarm Iraq if necessary. In mid-October the U.S. Congress supported Bush's stance by authorizing the president to use military force against Iraq, although lawmakers urged Bush to exhaust all diplomatic options first.

As the threat of American military action increased, Iraq agreed to allow the UN weapons inspectors to return "without conditions." In November the UN Security Council responded to Bush's calls for action by unanimously (with the agreement of all) passing a new resolution regarding Iraq. Resolution 1441 declared Iraq in violation of earlier UN resolutions, authorized a new round of weapons inspections, and promised that Iraq would face "serious consequences" if it failed to comply.

Weapons inspectors from the United Nations Monitoring, Verification, and Inspection Commission (UN-MOVIC), led by Hans Blix (1928–) of Sweden, returned to

Iraq on November 18, 2002. Their reports over the next few months were mixed. Sometimes Iraqi authorities were very cooperative. At other times, however, they seemed to be hiding information from the inspectors. The Bush administration was dissatisfied with Blix's reports and continued to pressure the UN Security Council to authorize the use of military force to disarm Iraq and remove Hussein from power.

On February 5, 2003, Powell appeared before the UN Security Council to make the United States' case against Iraq. He presented evidence that he claimed proved Iraq still possessed weapons of mass destruction, including chemical and biological weapons. He also argued that Hussein was determined to build nuclear weapons. "We have no indication that Saddam Hussein has ever abandoned his nuclear weapons program," Powell stated, as quoted by *Online NewsHour*. "On the contrary, we have more than a decade of proof that he remains determined to acquire nuclear weapons."

Hans Blix, executive chairman of the United Nations Monitoring, Verification, and Inspection Commission sent to Iraq to look for weapons of mass destruction. *Photograph by Mark Lennihan. AP/Wide World Photos. Reproduced by permission.*

Powell presented spy photos of suspected weapons facilities in Iraq, tape recordings of intercepted telephone conversations between Iraqi officials, and statements from informants inside Hussein's government. He accused Iraq of following a policy of "evasion and deception" for a dozen years, intentionally hiding evidence of weapons programs from UN inspectors. Finally, he suggested that a link existed between Hussein and the Al Qaeda terrorist group, despite the widely accepted argument that the highly religious Al Qaeda would never work with Hussein's secular (nonreligious) government. On the basis of his evidence, Powell insisted that the Security Council pass a new resolution authorizing its members to use force to disarm Iraq. "We must not shrink from whatever is ahead of us. We must not fail in our duty and our responsibility for the citizens of the countries that are represented by this body," he said. "Leaving Saddam

Hussein in possession of weapons of mass destruction for a few more months or years is not an option, not in a post–September 11 world."

A diplomatic battle in the United Nations

Powell needed to persuade nine of the fourteen other member countries of the UN Security Council, including the four other permanent members, to vote in favor of a new resolution. But several members of the Security Council, especially France and Russia, still had doubts about the use of force against Iraq. They did not believe that Iraq posed an immediate threat and wanted to give the weapons inspectors more time to complete their work.

All fourteen members of the UN Security Council made statements in response to Powell's presentation. Several countries made it clear that they still did not support the use of force against Iraq. "The use of force can only be a final recourse," said French foreign minister Dominique de Villepin (1953–), as quoted by *Online NewsHour*. "We must move on to a new stage and further strengthen the inspections." Chinese foreign minister Tang Jiaxuan (1938–) argued that the inspections should continue as long as there was "the slightest hope for political settlement."

But several other member nations expressed support for a new resolution. They agreed that Powell's evidence showed that Iraq was not complying with Resolution 1441, and they said the UN must be willing to back up its resolutions with force. British foreign secretary Jack Straw (1946–) noted that Hussein appeared to be "gambling that we will lose our nerve rather than enforce our will." Spanish foreign minister Ana Palacio (1948–) felt it was clear that Iraq was not cooperating with the UN inspectors, adding, "Inspectors are not detectives, they are [there] to witness the voluntary disarmament of Iraq."

The UN Security Council also heard from Mohammed Aldouri (1942–), Iraq's ambassador to the United Nations. Aldouri claimed that Powell's information was wrong and accused the Bush administration of manufacturing evidence. He denied that Iraq possessed weapons of mass destruction and insisted that there was no relationship between Hussein and Al Qaeda. "There are incorrect allegations [accusations], unnamed sources, unknown sources," Aldouri said, as quoted by *Online NewsHour.* "The pronouncements in Mr. Powell's statements on weapons of mass destruction are utterly unrelated to the truth…. Iraq is totally free of weapons of mass destruction—a statement repeated by numerous Iraqi officials for over a decade." In mid-February Blix issued a report in which he challenged Powell's claims and noted Iraq's recent cooperation with the weapons inspections.

Bush pushes ahead with war plans

Despite the lack of UN support, Bush was determined to proceed with a war to disarm Iraq and remove Hussein from power. In early 2003 he began sending hundreds of thousands of U.S. troops to the Persian Gulf. Bush received support from Great Britain and a few other countries, though many other nations opposed his plan.

Secretary of State Colin Powell tried to persuade members of the UN Security Council that Iraqi president Saddam Hussein was still a threat to the world. *Photograph by Scott Applewhite. AP/Wide World Photos. Reproduced by permission.*

On March 16 the United States, Great Britain, Spain, and Portugal announced that they would make one final push for a UN resolution. They wanted the Security Council to issue a clear ultimatum (final threat) to Hussein, stating that Iraq would be disarmed by force if it failed to comply with Resolution 1441 by a specific deadline. "Without a credible [believable] ultimatum authorizing force in the event of noncompliance, then more discussion is just more delay, with Saddam Hussein remaining armed with weapons of mass destruction and continuing a brutal murderous regime in Iraq," British prime minister Tony Blair (1953–) argued, as quoted by *Online NewsHour.*

In the tense discussions that followed, it became clear that France would veto any resolution authorizing the use of force against Iraq. Since France was a permanent member of

Iraq's ambassador to the United Nations Mohammed Aldouri (right) talks to a member of his delegation before addressing the UN Security Council.
©AFP/Corbis. Reproduced by permission.

the Security Council, its "no" vote would automatically prevent the resolution from passing. (All five permanent members of the council have veto power over resolutions.) The United States and its allies then decided not to seek a vote on a new resolution. They were worried that if the resolution authorizing the use of force failed to pass, some members of the international community would argue that any later military action was illegal under international law. Instead, they argued that the use of force was justified under previous UN resolutions. They claimed that Iraq was in violation of UN Resolution 1441, which promised "serious consequences" for noncompliance.

A number of members of the international community expressed outrage at the Bush administration's determination to act against the will of the UN Security Council. Led by French President Jacques Chirac (1932–), these critics argued that UN weapons inspections were effective in disarming Iraq and preventing Hussein from posing an immediate threat.

They also claimed that by invading Iraq, the United States would be defying international law, reducing the power of the United Nations, and increasing political instability around the world. "Nobody is supporting Saddam Hussein," said Canadian foreign minister Bill Graham. "But everyone recognizes in international politics you have to have a process where, before you invade a sovereign [independent] country, there has to be a reason for it, or we are going to lead to international chaos." The Arab League (an alliance of twenty Arab nations and the Palestine Liberation Organization that promotes political, military, and economic cooperation in the Arab world) issued a statement rejecting military action against Iraq and calling for economic sanctions to be lifted.

On March 17, 2003, Bush gave Hussein and his sons, Uday and Qusay, two days to leave Iraq or face a military invasion. This announcement ended six months of diplomacy aimed at securing UN support for the use of force against Iraq. "All the decades of deceit and cruelty have now reached an end. Saddam Hussein and his sons must leave Iraq within 48 hours. Their refusal to do so will result in military conflict commenced [begun] at a time of our choosing," Bush said, as quoted in *Online NewsHour*. Bush also restated his belief that Iraq represented a serious threat to world security. "The danger is clear. Using chemical, biological, or, one day, nuclear weapons obtained with the help of Iraq, the terrorists could fulfill their stated ambitions and kill thousands or hundreds of thousands of innocent people in our country or any other," he declared. "Instead of drifting along toward tragedy, we will set a course toward safety."

But Hussein remained defiant in the face of war. He called the accusations that Iraq possessed weapons of mass destruction a "great lie." He also warned that an attack against Iraq might lead to terrible consequences around the

British prime minister Tony Blair was a great supporter of the Bush administration's argument that military force was needed against Iraq. *Getty Images. Reproduced by permission.*

The Bush Doctrine

U.S. President George W. Bush justified the 2003 invasion of Iraq on the basis of a sweeping new foreign policy doctrine (a statement of basic governmental principles). The Bush Doctrine, as the new policy was called, held that the United States had the right to address perceived threats to its security or interests preemptively. In other words, the Bush administration argued that the United States had the right to attack another country in order to prevent a possible future war, even if that country had not yet made any aggressive moves toward the United States. Many people considered this to be a radical change in U.S. foreign policy, since in all previous wars the United States had acted only in response to an actual attack against the United States or its allies.

The Bush Doctrine was first developed after September 11, 2001, when terrorists attacked the United States. Afterward, Bush met with his top advisors in Camp David, Maryland, and outlined a series of phases in a global war against terrorism. The first phase involved a military strike against the people directly responsible for the September 11 attacks: Osama bin Laden and his Al Qaeda terrorist organization, and their protectors in Afghanistan, the Taliban government. In the second phase, Bush planned to extend the war on terrorism to include any group or nation that had the ability and desire to harm the United States.

Bush first described the new doctrine in his State of the Union address in January 2002. In this speech, he suggested that the old strategy of deterrence—maintaining a strong military in order to discourage other countries from attacking—was not effective against terrorists. He argued that the only way to defeat these new enemies was to strike first, destroying their ability to attack American interests before they could act. "At its most aggressive, this doctrine holds that the web of international institutions, alliances, and security arrangements ... that largely sustained United States foreign policy in the fifty years after World War II [1939–45] is no longer adequate in the face of shadowy global terrorist organizations and the states that aid or support them," Todd S. Purdum explained in *A Time of Our Choosing*.

Bush expanded on his new policy of preemption in June 2002, during a commencement speech at the U.S. Military Academy in West Point, New York. "If we wait for threats to fully materialize, we will have waited too long," he stated, as quoted in *The Iraq War Reader,* edited by Micah Sifry and Christopher Serf.

The war on terror will not be won on the defensive. We must take the battle to the enemy, disrupt his plans, and confront the worst threats before they emerge. In the world we have entered, the only path to safety is the path of action. And this nation will act…. All nations that decide for aggression and terror will pay a price. We will not leave the safety of America and the peace of the planet at the mercy of a few mad terrorists and tyrants. We will lift this dark threat from our country and from the world.

In the months leading up to the 2003 Iraq War, the Bush Doctrine came under intense criticism both within the United States and around the world. Opponents questioned the wisdom of the policy as well as its legality under international law. Critics pointed out that although enemies of the United States might possess weapons of mass destruction, there was no way to be certain they ever intended to use them. Some world leaders expressed strong reservations about the U.S. government using its military power preemptively.

When the United States launched its attack against Iraq in March 2003, many analysts viewed the war as a test case for the Bush Doctrine. American officials used the policy to justify going to war without the support of the United Nations and in the face of strong opposition around the world. Immediately after the war ended, Bush claimed that the policy had succeeded in eliminating Saddam Hussein as a threat to world peace. "All can know, friend and foe alike," he said, as quoted in *A Time of Our Choosing*, "that our nation has a mission: We will answer threats to our security, and we will defend the peace."

Over the next six months, however, the postwar situation in Iraq raised significant doubts about the effectiveness of the Bush Doctrine. Coalition troops struggled to maintain security in the face of Iraqi resistance, and a massive and expensive search failed to uncover any weapons of mass destruction in Iraq, which had been Bush's main justification for going to war. Some critics suggested that the Bush administration should have waited to gather more reliable intelligence (information collected through spying) before starting a war. "If preemption was justified as the best way to stop terrorists or rogue nations from acquiring devastatingly destructive weapons, everything depended on being able to ascertain [find out], swiftly and correctly, how determined such nations and groups were to get such weapons, and how close they were to having them," Purdum explained. "The experience in Iraq showed how hard it was to know for certain what the threats might be."

Sources: *Purdum, Todd S., and the staff of the New York Times.* A Time of Our Choosing: America's War in Iraq. *New York: Times Books, 2003; Sifry, Micah L., and Christopher Serf, eds.* The Iraq War Reader. *New York: Simon and Schuster, 2003.*

world. "When an enemy starts a large-scale battle, he must realize that the battle between us will be open wherever there is sky, land, and water in the entire world," he stated, as quoted in *Online NewsHour.*

The Iraq War creates controversy

Though the majority of Americans supported President Bush's decision to go to war against Iraq, it created controversy in the United States and in much of the world. The new conflict, which became known as the Iraq War or Gulf War II, marked the first time in history that the United States had launched a preemptive attack, meaning that it attacked a nation in order to prevent a possible future war, rather than in response to an attack by that nation against the United States or its interests. This policy of preemptive war became known as the Bush Doctrine (see box).

Much opposition to the Iraq War centered on Bush's decision to act without the support of the United Nations. Many critics argued that by acting alone, the U.S. government had reduced the power of the United Nations and alienated some of its closest allies. "We are really appalled by any country, whether it is a superpower or a poor country, that goes outside the United Nations and attacks independent countries," said former South African President Nelson Mandela (1918–), as quoted in *War Plan Iraq* by Milan Rai. "No country should be allowed to take the law into its own hands.... What they [the Bush administration] are introducing is chaos in international affairs and we condemn that in the strongest terms."

Some critics complained that there was not enough evidence to prove that Iraq posed a threat to world security. Others worried that the war would increase anti-American feelings throughout the world and lead to more terrorist attacks. The Church of England released a statement, quoted in *War Plan Iraq,* that said: "No convincing evidence has been presented to support the argument that Iraq is rebuilding its weapons of mass destruction program, or that Iraq poses an immediate threat to regional and international security. An attack on another Muslim country [in addition to Afghanistan], particularly one with no proven link to the September 11 atrocities, would be taken by many as evidence of an inbuilt hostility to the Muslim world." Finally, some accused Bush of pursuing the war either out of personal hatred toward Hussein, who allegedly had once tried to have Bush's father murdered, or because he wanted to control Iraq's vast oil reserves.

In the days leading up to the start of the war, large-scale antiwar demonstrations erupted around the world. An estimated 200,000 people marched down Broadway in New York City, carrying banners and shouting "No blood for oil!" A record 1,350 protesters were arrested in San Francisco for blocking intersections, smashing police-car windows, and vomiting on the sidewalk to show how sick the war made them. Rallies and marches took place on college campuses across the United States as well as in 350 cities around the world, including Berlin, Paris, and Cairo. An estimated 750,000 people rallied in Hyde Park in London to protest Blair's decision to support Bush.

The Bush administration did not waver from its position, however. It continued to argue that the United States was going to war to free the Iraqi people from a brutal dictator and to defend the world from a grave and immediate danger. The administration and its supporters claimed that replacing Hussein with a democratic government would bring peace and prosperity to Iraq and a new stability to the Middle East.

A protestor against another war with Iraq marches outside of the White House. Her Marine husband is about to be deployed to the Persian Gulf region. *Photograph by Rick Bowmer. AP/Wide World Photos. Reproduced by permission.*

Operation Iraqi Freedom, March 2003

10

For more than a year, the United States tried to persuade the United Nations (UN) to authorize the use of military force to disarm Iraq and remove Iraqi President Saddam Hussein (1937–) from power. By early 2003 it became clear that these diplomatic efforts had failed. But U.S. President George W. Bush (1946–) was determined to go to war against Iraq, even without UN support. He claimed that Iraq possessed weapons of mass destruction and posed a significant threat to world security. He insisted that military action was necessary to free the Iraqi people from a brutal dictator and to defend the world from grave danger.

On March 17, 2003, Bush gave Hussein and his two sons, Uday and Qusay, forty-eight hours to leave Iraq or face a U.S.-led military invasion. The Iraqi leader ignored the warning, and the 2003 Iraq War (also known as Gulf War II) began two days later. From the beginning, the main focus of the war was removing Hussein from power. American military leaders felt that toppling Hussein would create chaos in the Iraqi army and decrease its ability to fight. The planners of the war also believed that the Iraqi people would welcome the U.S. troops once they realized that Hussein's reign of terror was over.

The world moves toward war

During the forty-eight-hour period following Bush's final warning, Hussein remained defiant. The Iraqi leader claimed that the United States was plotting to steal Iraq's oil reserves and force its will on the Middle East. He encouraged the Iraqi people to resist the coming invasion in any way possible. He also sent his sons to a bank in downtown Baghdad to withdraw one billion dollars in cash, or about one-quarter of Iraq's total currency reserves.

Under the Bush administration's original plan, the Iraq War was supposed to start with a rapid push of ground troops into Iraq from the tiny country of Kuwait to the south. These troops would move northwest toward Baghdad as quickly as possible to trap Hussein's government in the capital city. One column of troops—the U.S. Army's Third Infantry Division, led by Lieutenant General William Wallace—would move swiftly through the desert on the west side of the Euphrates River. In the meantime, fifty thousand U.S. troops from the First Marine Expeditionary Force, under the command of Lieutenant General James T. Conway, would move in a parallel path to the east, up the valley between the Euphrates and Tigris Rivers. The second phase of the war would involve a massive air assault designed to create "shock and awe" among the enemy forces and persuade them to surrender. As it turned out, however, the war began in an entirely different way.

Sometime in the two days following Bush's ultimatum, the U.S. government received information on the location of Hussein and other senior Iraqi officials. They were believed to be hiding in underground bunkers (fortified structures) at the home of Hussein's daughter, near Baghdad University. The intelligence (information gained from spying) came from several different sources and appeared to be accurate. After talking with his top advisors, Bush decided to act on the information. He realized that ordering an air strike would be dangerous because American pilots would have to fly through the middle of Iraqi air defenses, but he saw it as a possible opportunity to end the war before it even began by killing Hussein and his top officials.

A "decapitation attack"

On March 20, about ninety minutes after Bush's ultimatum ran out, the U.S. military launched a massive bombing strike with the intention of killing Hussein. Military officials called it a "decapitation attack," because its aim was to destroy the head of the Iraqi government. "We want to turn the Iraqi military into a chicken with its head cut off," one senior U.S. Navy official explained to *Time* magazine.

In the early morning hours over Baghdad, U.S. Navy ships stationed in the Persian Gulf and the Red Sea (a long, narrow sea that stretches along Saudi Arabia's western border) fired dozens of Tomahawk missiles, each equipped with a 1,000-pound (450-kilogram) warhead, at three targets in Baghdad. Warplanes immediately followed up with 2,000-pound (900-kilogram) "bunker-buster" bombs designed to destroy underground facilities. The attacks completely de-

Iraqi President Saddam Hussein (center) with his sons Uday (left) and Qusay (right). On March 17, 2003, George W. Bush gave Hussein and his two sons forty-eight hours to leave Iraq or face a U.S.-led military invasion. *Karim Sahib/AFP/Getty Images. Reproduced by permission.*

stroyed their intended targets. Intelligence reports indicated that some top Iraqi officials were killed in the assault, but it was unclear whether Hussein was among them.

Two hours later, Bush appeared on national television to announce the start of the military campaign, code named Operation Iraqi Freedom. "American and coalition forces are in the early stages of military operations to disarm Iraq, to free its people, and to defend the world from grave danger," he stated, as quoted by *Online NewsHour*. "On my orders, coalition forces have begun striking selected targets of military importance to undermine Saddam Hussein's ability to wage war. These are [the] opening stages of what will be a broad and concerted [intense] campaign."

A short time later Hussein appeared on Iraqi television to read a statement. He called the attack "a shameful crime" and pledged that "we will confront the invaders." American officials were quick to point out that Hussein's appearance did not necessarily mean that he had survived the "decapitation attack." They said that the statement could have been taped earlier or could have been read by one of the several "body doubles," men who closely resembled the Iraqi leader,—that Hussein sometimes used to stand in for him at public appearances.

Coalition ground forces enter Iraq

By the beginning of Operation Iraqi Freedom, the number of American military troops in the Persian Gulf region had reached 242,000. This was less than half as many as were deployed there during the 1991 Persian Gulf War. Some U.S. troops had remained in the region during the dozen years between the wars. American forces manned air bases in Saudi Arabia, for example, and U.S. Navy warships were stationed in the Persian Gulf. But most of the American ground troops were sent to the Middle East specifically to take part in Operation Iraqi Freedom. Around 130,000 were stationed in Kuwait, along Iraq's southern border.

Although Bush's decision to go to war against Iraq was not supported by the United Nations, the United States still managed to gain some assistance from thirty-five countries. Great Britain was the strongest supporter of Bush's in-

vasion of Iraq. British leaders sent 45,000 troops to aid the coalition, about the same number they had sent during the 1991 war. Other contributors of troops included Australia, with 18,000, and Poland, with 2,000. The other members of the coalition provided various forms of assistance, ranging from financial support to military equipment and intelligence. The coalition faced an estimated 375,000 Iraqi military, significantly less than the 1 million soldiers Iraq had to draw upon in the 1991 conflict.

Shortly after the first bombs hit Baghdad as part of the "decapitation attack," Iraqi army units began firing missiles toward the U.S. and British troops that were gathered along the Kuwaiti border. Although the missiles missed their targets, they still caused considerable problems for the coalition forces. Each time a warning siren sounded, the troops raced to put on hot, heavy protective suits in case the missiles carried chemical weapons. They had to wear these suits until an all-clear signal sounded.

President Bush appearing on national television to announce the start of Operation Iraqi Freedom.
©Brooks Kraft/Corbis.
Reproduced by permission.

News Coverage of the 2003 Iraq War

The live television news coverage of the 1991 Persian Gulf War amazed viewers around the world with dramatic scenes of bombing campaigns and ground combat. It marked the first time that ordinary people had experienced a military conflict so immediately. But news coverage of the 2003 Iraq War went beyond the high expectations that the previous conflict had created.

In 1991 most journalists had to report on the action from a distance. The correspondents in Baghdad watched the start of the air war from their hotel balconies as Iraqi "minders" hovered close by. These Iraqi security personnel controlled the reporters' access to people and places as well as the content of their stories. Most other reporters filed their stories from neighboring Saudi Arabia. The U.S. military did not allow journalists to accompany troops into battle because they worried that it would create a security risk. As a result, the press was forced to wait on the sidelines for U.S. military officials to update them on developments.

Journalists covering the 2003 Iraq War had a much broader set of options to choose from. Prior to the start of the 2003 conflict, coalition leaders invited major news organizations to "embed" correspondents within American and British military units, with the understanding that their reports would be made available to other news organizations. The nine hundred journalists and photographers who chose this option joined their units for training several weeks before the war began. When the fighting started, the correspondents traveled into Iraq along with their units and reported on the action as it occurred.

The new policy of allowing embedded reporters in military units offered a number of advantages for news organizations. Embedded reporters were able to travel into the war zone under the protection of coalition troops and provide the public with eyewitness accounts of the planning and execution of major military campaigns. Some people worried that the military would censor the reports of embedded journalists. As it happened, however, coalition leaders rarely found it necessary. Most journalists carefully avoided giving away any information that might put their units in danger.

Many news organizations chose to embed some correspondents and send others to cover the war independently as "unilaterals." For example, Reuters sent seventy correspondents to Iraq, thirty of them as embedded reporters and forty as unilaterals. The main advantage of operating independently was that these reporters were free to go wherever they wanted and report on whatever they saw. The main disadvantage was that they were unprotected by American forces and often faced great personal risks.

Some news organizations also stationed correspondents in Baghdad. Saddam Hussein's government granted visas to most reporters who requested permission to cover the war from the Iraqi capital. The Iraqi government welcomed news coverage because it believed that pictures of bombing damage and civilian casualties would arouse worldwide sympathy. But the reporters in Baghdad faced a number of problems. Their movements were strictly limited by Iraqi minders. Coalition leaders also were concerned that the Iraqi regime might use the reporters as "human shields" to protect potential bombing targets, as had happened during the 1991 war.

Finally, some news organizations stationed correspondents in the small country of Qatar, east of Saudi Arabia, where coalition leaders set up a media center to relay official information about the conflict. These reporters received regular updates on combat operations and casualties. They were also the first to gain access to photos and video footage shot by coalition soldiers. For example, they saw the dramatic rescue of U.S. prisoner of war Private Jessica Lynch (1983–) and watched U.S. Marines conduct a raid on Hussein's "Green Palace."

The variety of options available for news organizations covering the war meant that audiences around the world received remarkably close looks at many aspects of the conflict. Television viewers saw vivid pictures of explosions and fires lighting up the sky over Baghdad, images of British forces fighting for control of Basra, and dramatic footage of American tanks rolling through the streets of the Iraqi capital. But such images came at a cost: A total of twenty journalists and photographers died during the war, three in Baghdad and seventeen elsewhere in Iraq. Not all of the deaths resulted from combat, but the majority of those that did were "friendly fire" incidents at the hands of American forces.

Although the news coverage of the Iraq War received a great deal of praise, it also generated some criticism. Some people complained that the embedded reporters, with their breathless accounts of combat, gave viewers the impression that the Iraqi resistance was stronger than it actually was, while others worried that the practice of "embedding" would bias the reporters' coverage in favor of the soldiers they had trained and traveled with. Other critics claimed that the emphasis on live action left little time for analyzing and interpreting the stories, leaving viewers without context for what they were seeing. Reporters sometimes followed events closely even when they had little bearing on the overall conflict. In the meantime some parts of the war, like the contributions made by Special Operations forces, went unreported. Finally, some news organizations that had adopted editorial positions either opposing or supporting the war were accused of providing biased coverage.

Sources: Fletcher, Kim. "The Media War." In Rooney, Ben. The Daily Telegraph War on Saddam: The Complete Story of the Iraq Campaign. *London: Robinson, 2003.*

This situation helped persuade U.S. military leaders to launch the ground invasion of Iraq on March 20, a full day ahead of schedule. Led by the U.S. Army Third Infantry Division and British Marines, more than two thousand tanks, armored vehicles, trucks, and artillery crossed over the Kuwaiti border north into Iraq. To their surprise, they encountered very little organized resistance as they moved north toward Basra, the second-largest city in Iraq. Instead of the entrenched Iraqi army forces they had faced in the 1991 war, they encountered only small pockets of hostile fire.

By the end of the first day of fighting, coalition forces had captured the port city of Umm Qasr on the Persian Gulf. They immediately began clearing the harbor of mines (underwater explosive devices) so it could receive shipments of medicine, food, and other humanitarian aid for the people of Iraq. They also secured many of the one thousand oil wells in southern Iraq so Iraqi forces could not sabotage them. Iraqi troops only managed to set fire to nine wells, as opposed to the six hundred Kuwaiti wells they had set ablaze during the 1991 conflict.

"Shock and awe" bombing campaign begins

On March 21 the U.S.-led coalition launched its "shock and awe" bombing campaign. Over the course of the war, a total of thirty thousand coalition bombs and missiles would rain down on strategic targets in Iraq. In the first attack on Baghdad, bombs exploded every ten seconds for three hours. The main targets included government buildings, command and control centers for the Iraqi military, and suspected weapons facilities. One bombing raid destroyed Hussein's Republican Palace, located on the bank of the Tigris River in Baghdad. Coalition warplanes also attacked cities in northern Iraq, including Tikrit, Mosul, and Kirkuk.

The idea behind the coalition's overwhelming air assault was to weaken Hussein's hold on power and persuade the Iraqi people to surrender. "We are seeing an awfully impressive display of our ability to bring very large numbers of important strategic targets under attack at the same time," said retired Air Force Colonel John Warden, as quoted by *Online NewsHour*. "I would find it very difficult to conceive of how those utterly

critical internal security organizations, the things on which Saddam Hussein depends, ... could really be functioning and could maintain the degree of repression [control through the use of intimidation and force] that they need to."

An estimated eight thousand Iraqi army soldiers surrendered to coalition forces during the first few days of the war. But others simply took off their uniforms and melted into the civilian population. Some experts worried that these former soldiers might later organize small bands of resistance fighters and attack coalition forces using the tactics of guerrilla warfare (an unconventional fighting style that uses methods like ambushes, booby traps, and sniper attacks).

U.S. Marines from the 1st Marine Division pass a sign pointing the way to Baghdad as they continue their march to the capital of Iraq. *Photograph by Joe Raedle. Getty Images. Reproduced by permission.*

"Wave of steel" advances toward Baghdad

As the "shock and awe" bombing campaign got underway, U.S. ground troops continued to push deeper into

Iraqi territory. In his book *War on Saddam,* Ben Rooney called it "the fastest armored advance in the history of modern warfare." The ground forces encountered their first significant enemy fire outside cities in southern Iraq, including Samawah and Nasiriyah. Some of the fire came from Iraqi army units, but a surprising amount came from paramilitary fighters and irregular forces (fighters who are not part of a formal army).

On March 22 the U.S. Army's Third Infantry and V Corps came under attack by Iraqi forces that were dug in to defend Nasiriyah. This city marked a strategic point on the road to Baghdad, 200 miles (322 kilometers) northwest, because it contained two important bridges across the Euphrates River. The coalition forces wanted to push onward toward Baghdad as quickly as possible, so they did not plan to occupy Nasiriyah. But they did need to capture a critical bridge over the Euphrates so they could use it to transport troops and equipment to the Iraqi capital.

During the Battle of Nasiriyah, the coalition troops came under heavy enemy artillery fire. They responded by calling in air strikes against the Iraqi forces. The coalition air power overwhelmed the Iraqis and persuaded many of them to surrender. After capturing the bridge, the Third Infantry continued rolling across the desert toward Baghdad in what one reporter described as a 20-mile (32-kilometer) "wave of steel." They got within 100 miles (160 kilometers) of the capital after only three days of fighting.

Iraqi forces use illegal tactics

When the "wave of steel" had moved on, however, the Iraqi resistance grew more intense. On March 23 a group of five thousand U.S. Marines that had been left to defend the bridge near Nasiriyah engaged in a major firefight with Iraqi forces. U.S. Army Lieutenant General John Abizaid (1951–), speaking from the U.S. Central Command (CENTCOM) facility in Qatar, described it as the "sharpest engagement" of the war so far. By the time the city was securely in coalition hands, more than thirty American soldiers had been killed and sixty more wounded.

Over several days of fighting, the Iraqi forces showed their willingness to use whatever tactics were necessary to

oppose the Americans, even if those tactics violated the basic rules of war. For example, several groups of Iraqi soldiers approached U.S. troops under a flag of surrender and then attacked them. In addition, some of the Iraqi forces in Nasiriyah used a hospital as a base of operations for their attacks against the coalition (medical personnel and facilities are generally considered neutral in wartime). Other Iraqi fighters used women as shields or fired on American troops from mosques (Muslim places of worship).

The Iraqi strategy seemed to focus on confusing, disrupting, and harassing the coalition forces to delay their march toward Baghdad. Though banned under international law, these tactics allowed even small Iraqi forces to have an impact. They also proved very difficult for the coalition forces to defend against. After all, the coalition was following accepted rules of engagement that were designed to protect civilians (people not involved in a war, including women and children) and their property.

An American prisoner of war (POW) being displayed on Iraqi television. U.S. leaders claimed that showing POWs on television violated the Geneva Conventions.
©Reuters NewMedia Inc./Corbis. Reproduced by permission.

The U.S.-led coalition received another jolt of bad news on March 23 when a U.S. Army supply convoy was captured by Iraqi forces. The convoy apparently took a wrong turn and was ambushed by Fedayeen paramilitary fighters (a group of Iraqi fighters that was intensely loyal to Saddam Hussein) dressed in civilian clothes. Twelve American soldiers were lost in the raid. Five of them later were displayed on Iraqi television as prisoners of war, and most of the rest were killed. U.S. leaders criticized Iraq's decision to show footage of the prisoners, claiming that this violated the Geneva Conventions (a series of international treaties intended to guarantee the humane treatment of enemy soldiers and prisoners and the protection of civilians during war). But some Muslim nations pointed out that the U.S. government had refused to grant the protections of the Geneva Conventions to Al Qaeda fighters who were captured in Afghanistan, labeling them terrorists rather than soldiers. (Al Qaeda is a radical Islamic terrorist group responsible for the September 11, 2001, attacks against the United States.)

The two leaders appeal to their forces

On March 25 Hussein issued another statement through Iraqi television, appealing to his people to band together to fight the invaders. "They came to dishonor your land and honor," he stated, as quoted by *CNN.com.* "Today is your turn to show your pure Arab heritage, your courage fighting on every road and every land." A short time later coalition forces hit the Iraqi television station with a Tomahawk missile. The strike knocked out the TV signal and disrupted Hussein's ability to command and control his forces.

Bush responded to Hussein's statement with a speech at the Pentagon (the headquarters of the U.S. military) in Arlington, Virginia. He criticized Iraq's fighting tactics, praised the coalition's performance, and assured the American people that victory was near. "Our coalition is on a steady advance. We're making good progress," he stated, as quoted by *CNN.com.*

> We're fighting an enemy that knows no rules of law, that will wear civilian uniforms, that are willing to kill in order to continue the reign of fear of Saddam Hussein, but we're fighting them with bravery and courage. We cannot know the duration of this war; yet we know its outcome. We will prevail. The Iraqi regime will be disarmed. The Iraqi regime will be ended. The

Iraqi people will be free. And our world will be more secure and peaceful.

Bush also outlined a request for the U.S. Congress to authorize $75 billion in emergency spending to help pay for the war.

In the meantime, the American "wave of steel" advanced to within 60 miles (97 kilometers) of Baghdad. The coalition ground forces engaged in a battle near Najaf in the Euphrates River valley. The fighting took place during a sandstorm (a desert windstorm that blows up huge clouds of sand), which prevented the coalition from calling in air strikes against enemy positions. At the same time, coalition forces began trying to secure areas in both southern and northern Iraq. British forces began fighting for control of the southern city of Basra, while paratroopers (soldiers who descend into a war zone by parachutes) from the U.S. Army's 173rd Airborne Division were dropped into northern Iraq to secure an airfield for coalition use.

Iraqi leader Saddam Hussein issuing a statement through Iraqi television, appealing to his people to band together to fight the invaders. *©Reuters NewMedia Inc./Corbis. Reproduced by permission.*

Critics question Bush's war plan

On March 28 the American officer in charge of the ground war, General Wallace, gave an interview to the *Washington Post*. In the article, he discussed the surprising intensity of resistance that coalition forces had encountered. He admitted that the coalition's war plan had not addressed some of the situations his troops had faced. "The enemy we're fighting is different from the one we'd war-gamed against, because of these paramilitary forces," he said, as quoted in *A Time of Our Choosing* by Todd Purdum. "We knew they were here, but we did not know how they would fight." Wallace also expressed his concern that the war might last longer than planners assumed and require additional troops.

When the American media picked up on Wallace's comments, newspapers and television news programs were suddenly full of experts questioning the Bush administration's war plan. Reporters pointed to a number of accidents and problems that had occurred in the early days of the war as examples of the coalition's poor preparation. For example, seven coalition soldiers were killed when two British helicopters collided in midair. A U.S. Patriot missile mistakenly shot down a British Tornado attack plane returning from a mission, killing its pilot and navigator. Members of the U.S. 101st Airborne Division stationed in Kuwait were shocked when one of their own men, a Muslim sergeant with a history of disciplinary problems, threw hand grenades into two tents full of sleeping commanders. Two U.S. officers were killed and fourteen others were wounded in the attack.

Administration officials dismissed the claim that the Iraqi resistance was unexpected and tried to reassure the public that the war was proceeding on schedule. General Richard Myers, chairman of the Joint Chiefs of Staff (a group of top military advisors to the president of the United States, consisting of a chairman and the chief of each branch of the armed services), argued that questioning the war plan had a negative effect on troops in the field. "It is not helpful to have those kind of comments come out when we've got troops in combat, because, first of all, they're false, they're absolutely wrong, they bear no resemblance to the truth, and it's just harmful to our troops that are out there fighting very bravely, very courageously," he stated, as quoted by *Online NewsHour*.

Overall, most analysts seemed pleased with the coalition's rapid push toward Baghdad. But some experts expressed concern about what the troops might encounter once they reached the Iraqi capital. They expected Baghdad to be guarded by highly trained soldiers from Iraq's Republican Guard (an elite, one-hundred-thousand-man force that was the best-trained and best-equipped part of Iraq's army). They worried that coalition ground troops might face a long and bloody fight to capture the city. Instead of the "cakewalk" that some Bush administration insiders had predicted, they worried that the war might turn into months of costly combat.

As the war entered its second week, a series of incidents raised concerns about its effect on civilians. Heavy air

strikes continued to hit Baghdad, especially government targets and Republican Guard units protecting the capital. The coalition reportedly used eight thousand precision-guided missiles during the last twelve days of March. On March 27 Iraqi officials claimed that one of these bombs hit a busy Baghdad market, killing fifteen civilians. American leaders said the market was not a target and blamed Iraqi surface-to-air missiles or fallout from antiaircraft guns.

On March 29 an Iraqi suicide bomber killed four U.S. soldiers at a military checkpoint near Najaf. Two days later U.S. soldiers fired into a van that failed to stop at the checkpoint. It turned out that the van was carrying thirteen women and children, seven of whom were killed. A U.S. military spokesman insisted that the American soldiers had followed proper military procedure in the incident. But the episode highlighted the growing conflict between the Iraqi people and the foreign soldiers who were supposedly there to liberate them.

Smoke rising over the Iraqi capital of Baghdad after explosions rocked the city.
©Reuters NewMedia Inc./Corbis. Reproduced by permission.

The Fall of Baghdad, April 2003

11

During the first two weeks of the 2003 Iraq War, the U.S.-led coalition's "wave of steel" ground assault advanced quickly toward the Iraqi capital of Baghdad. The coalition also launched an intensive bombing campaign designed to create "shock and awe" among enemy forces and persuade them to surrender. From the beginning of the war, coalition troops faced less organized resistance from the Iraqi army than they had expected. But they also received an unexpectedly hostile reception from the Iraqi people. In fact, they faced a surprising number of sneak attacks from irregular forces (fighters who are not part of a formal army) using the tactics of guerrilla warfare (an unconventional fighting style that uses methods like ambushes, booby traps, and sniper attacks). As the situation in Iraq grew more complex, the Bush administration faced increasing criticism of its war plan.

In early April the coalition forces prepared to fight for control of Baghdad. U.S. military officials worried that the troops might face stiff resistance from Iraqi Republican Guard forces, as well as the possibility of chemical weapons attacks, as they neared the capital. (The Republican Guard was an elite, one-hundred-thousand-man force that was the best-trained and best-equipped part of Iraq's army.) But the military campaign known as Operation Iraqi Freedom proceeded rapidly, as the coalition captured Saddam International Airport and surrounded Baghdad. The Iraqi capital fell to coalition forces on April 9, after only three weeks of combat. The capture of Baghdad was symbolized by the toppling of a large statue of Iraqi leader Saddam Hussein (1937–) in the capital's Firdos Square. Over the next week, coalition forces went on to capture Mosul and Tikrit in northern Iraq and secure the southern city of Basra. On May 1, 2003, U.S. President George W. Bush (1946–) made a historic speech in which he declared an end to major combat operations in Iraq. But some analysts warned that the most difficult task, "winning the peace," still lay ahead.

Coalition forces advance on Baghdad

At the end of March the Bush administration had faced growing criticism about its handling of the Iraq War. But the national mood changed on April 1, when U.S. Special Forces staged a dramatic rescue of U.S. Army Private Jessica Lynch (1983–), who was being held as a prisoner of war (POW) in Iraq. Lynch had been captured on March 23, following the ambush of her supply company by Iraqi Fedayeen forces. (The Fedayeen was a group of Iraqi paramilitary fighters that was intensely loyal to Saddam Hussein.) She suffered serious injuries in the ambush, and the Iraqis transported her to Saddam Hospital in Nasiriyah. An Iraqi lawyer whose wife worked at the hospital informed U.S. troops where Lynch was being held. She was rescued in a daring nighttime helicopter raid that involved Army Rangers, Navy SEALs, Marines, and Air Force pilots. The U.S. troops entered the hospital, found Lynch, and carried her out on a stretcher to a waiting helicopter. The rescue was captured on video and generated a great deal of positive media coverage.

In the meantime, the U.S. Army Third Infantry Division continued to face little organized resistance as it rolled toward Baghdad. But U.S. military leaders still worried that Iraqi Republican Guard forces would make a last, desperate attempt to protect the capital. The American planners drew a large, imaginary circle around Baghdad and called it the Red

Zone. This was where they expected the coalition forces to face the toughest resistance from Iraqi troops.

The most likely place for a showdown was the Karbala Gap, about 50 miles (80 kilometers) south of Baghdad. Coalition forces had to pass through this narrow, sandy plain between Lake Buhayrat and the Euphrates River during their final approach to the capital. U.S. Military Intelligence believed that the Republican Guard would use chemical weapons against the Third Infantry here. As the U.S. troops advanced, they were placed at a high level of chemical alert. All of the soldiers were required to wear hot, heavy protective suits and keep their gas masks and respirators close by.

The Third Infantry entered the Karbala Gap in the early morning hours of April 3. To their surprise, they continued to face only scattered resistance. They advanced quickly and reached the Euphrates River a half-day ahead of schedule, without suffering any casualties (killed or wounded sol-

U.S. Army soldiers move to secure the VIP terminal of Saddam International Airport during a dawn advance toward the Iraqi capital of Baghdad.
Photograph by Scott Nelson. Getty Images. Reproduced by permission.

diers). It appeared that the coalition's "shock and awe" bombing campaign had destroyed many Republican Guard units and forced others to retreat. Once the coalition forces passed safely through the Karbala Gap, Brigadier General Vincent Brooks told reporters, "The dagger is clearly pointed at the heart of the regime."

Troops reach Baghdad

On the evening of April 3 coalition forces began fighting for control of Saddam International Airport, about 12 miles (19 kilometers) outside Baghdad. Republican Guard troops defended the facility using tanks and artillery. The coalition forces hit the Republican Guard with air strikes and then smashed through the walls surrounding the airport with tanks and armored vehicles. By morning they had captured the final link between Hussein's government and the outside world. They renamed the facility Baghdad International Airport and began preparing to receive coalition military aircraft there.

Around the same time, U.S. Special Forces conducted a raid on Hussein's "Green Palace," the largest and most elaborate of the Iraqi president's seventy-eight homes. This compound covered more than 2 square miles (5 square kilometers) along the shore of Lake Tharthar, about 150 miles (240 kilometers) north of Baghdad. It was built in 1993, while economic sanctions were creating severe hardships for the Iraqi people, to demonstrate that Hussein was still in command following the 1991 Persian Gulf War. (Economic sanctions are trade restrictions intended to punish a country for breaking international law.) U.S. Central Command showed reporters a video of heavily armed Special Forces soldiers walking around the ornate palace and grounds. The video was intended to convince the Iraqi people that Hussein was powerless to stop the coalition forces.

By April 5, U.S. troops had surrounded the capital and started flying additional troops and supplies into Baghdad International Airport. In a show of force, a convoy of more than sixty tanks and armored vehicles rolled through the city's southern suburbs on a reconnaissance (information-gathering) mission. The idea behind the mission, which received the code name Operation Thunder Run, was to test

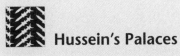

Hussein's Palaces

As president of Iraq, Saddam Hussein enjoyed the use of about seventy-eight ornate palaces. Many of these estates rivaled the world's most famous homes—such as England's Buckingham Palace and France's Château de Versailles—in size and grandeur. Hussein constructed these palaces to provide lasting monuments to himself and visible demonstrations of his power. Several of the palaces were built or rebuilt in the decade following the 1991 Persian Gulf War, while millions of ordinary Iraqis were suffering hardships under UN economic sanctions.

The world got its first glimpse inside Hussein's palaces after he was removed from power during the 2003 Iraq War. Coalition soldiers described gold-plated bathroom fixtures, European marble floors, crystal chandeliers, soaring cathedral ceilings, stained-glass windows, sweeping staircases, and ballrooms containing acres of parquet flooring. The presidential compounds were surrounded by elaborately landscaped grounds full of pools, waterfalls, man-made lakes, and aquariums connected by garden paths and stone bridges.

Hussein's regime used the palaces for many different purposes. Various palaces served as military compounds, government offices, housing for foreign visitors, and vacation homes for Iraqi leaders. The Radwaniyah palace, located west of Baghdad near Saddam International Airport, had a prison large enough to hold five thousand people. For many years, the U.S. government suspected that some of the palaces might also serve as hiding places for weapons of mass destruc-

tion, but Iraqi officials consistently refused to allow inspectors to search the compounds.

The largest of all of Hussein's palaces, covering 2.5 square miles (6.5 square kilometers) of land, was his official residence in his hometown of Tikrit. The second-largest was Maqar al Tharthar, commonly known as the "Green Palace," located between Baghdad and Tikrit. Built in 1993, it was known for its huge man-made lake and beautifully landscaped grounds. Another ornate palace was Qasr Shatt-al-Arab near Basra, also known as the "Pink Palace" because it was made of pale rose-colored stone. Hussein also maintained several palaces in Baghdad, including the Republican Palace, which covered 500 acres (2 square kilometers) along the Tigris River. This compound was destroyed in 2003 during the coalition's "shock and awe" bombing campaign.

During the 2003 Iraq War, coalition troops invaded many of Hussein's palaces and turned them into military command centers. Once the combat ended, bitter Iraqis attacked several of these symbols of Hussein's rule. They looted the palaces, stealing everything of value they could find, and damaged or destroyed the buildings and grounds.

Sources: Butcher, Tim. *"Palace Exposes Dictator's Gilded Tyranny."* Daily Telegraph, *April 8, 2003. Reprinted in Rooney, Ben.* The Daily Telegraph War on Saddam: The Complete Story of the Iraq Campaign. *London: Robinson, 2003; Thompson, Justin. "Saddam's Palaces."* CBC News Online, *April 7, 2003. Available online at http://www.cbc.ca/ news/iraq/issues_analysis/saddam_palaces.html (accessed on January 8, 2004).*

the Iraqi defenses. Many of the American vehicles were hit by enemy mortars and small-arms fire. The Iraqis attacked in pickup trucks mounted with machine guns. They also used cars, taxis, and even motorcycles with rifles tied to them. An estimated two thousand Iraqi resistance fighters were killed along the way, and twenty-five hundred Republican Guard troops surrendered. American casualties were light.

Despite all evidence to the contrary, Iraqi officials insisted that they were successfully resisting the American invasion. The main spokesman for Hussein's government was its information minister, Mohammed Said al-Sahhaf (1940–). Even as battles raged on the streets of Baghdad just a few hundred yards away, Sahhaf was telling reporters that there were no American troops within 100 miles (160 kilometers) of the city. "I reassure you Baghdad is safe," he insisted, as quoted in *War on Saddam* by Ben Rooney. "There is no presence of the American columns in the city of Baghdad. None at all." He apparently hoped to convince the Iraqi people that Hussein remained in control of the country. The international media began referring to Sahhaf as "Baghdad Bob" and "Comical Ali" because they found his claims so ridiculous.

British forces capture Basra

As U.S. troops closed in on Baghdad, British forces secured Iraq's second-largest city, the city of Basra in southern Iraq. On April 7, following two weeks of combined political and military operations, British leaders announced that they were in control of the city. Military experts praised the British troops for taking over the city gradually and winning the confidence of Basra's residents along the way. As the British soldiers convinced the people of Basra that Hussein's government could no longer threaten them, the people began showing their support for the coalition, even helping British troops root out Hussein's remaining loyalists. However, there also were outbreaks of looting, with residents breaking into shops, schools, and hotels and carrying off whatever they could find.

A key event in the capture of Basra was the reported death of one of the most hated members of Hussein's government, General Ali Hassan al-Majid (1941–). Majid earned the nickname "Chemical Ali" in 1988, when he allegedly ordered the use of chemical weapons against the Kurds (a non-Arab people of northern Iraq), killing an estimated five thousand people. He also oversaw Iraq's brutal occupation of Kuwait before the 1991 Persian Gulf War and led the Iraqi army forces that brutally crushed a Shiite Muslim uprising in southern Iraq after that war. (Sunni and Shiite are the two main branches of Islam. About 90 percent of all Muslims are Sunnis.) He later became governor of Basra Province, where he continued to use terror and violence to protect Hussein's interests. The people of Basra celebrated when British military leaders announced that "Chemical Ali" had likely been killed in a coalition air strike against his home. As it turned out, Majid survived the attack and went into hiding for several months. He was finally captured by coalition forces in August 2003.

When it became clear that Basra was in British hands, many of the city's residents expressed their appreciation for the coalition's efforts. "There were a couple of kids who came up to me and did high fives," said British Private Shahid Khan in *War on Saddam.* "It was a lovely gesture. I thought there was going to be a lot of resistance but now, it seems, it's going to be all right. The people have been brilliant. It's a very good day."

The fall of Baghdad

On April 8 coalition forces continued making reconnaissance missions through the streets of Baghdad. They took over several of Hussein's palaces and searched them for members of the Iraqi regime or documents relating to weapons programs. They also seized and held several strategic positions in the heart of the city. U.S. warplanes flew over the city constantly to provide support for the troops on the ground. Once again, coalition leaders were surprised that the troops faced only limited pockets of resistance. They encountered occasional small-arms fire from disorganized groups of fighters, but no battalions of Iraqi tanks or Republican Guard forces.

That evening, coalition forces launched another "decapitation attack" aimed at killing Iraqi President Saddam Hussein. (Decapitation means to cut off someone's head,—in this case, the head of the Iraqi government.) U.S. leaders had received intelligence (information from spying) indicating that Hussein, one of his sons, and several other senior government officials were meeting at a restaurant in the Mansur neighborhood of Baghdad. Coalition planes dropped "bunker-buster" bombs on the target, creating a 50-foot (15-meter) crater. Unfortunately, the air strikes also destroyed several nearby homes and killed several civilians (people not involved in a war, including women and children). American officials were at first hopeful the attack had killed Hussein, but British intelligence soon began receiving reports that the Iraqi leader was still alive.

Iraqis celebrate the fall of Hussein

Baghdad fell to coalition forces on April 9. American tanks moved through the city at will, and the Iraqi people finally began to believe that Hussein's rule had ended. John Daniszewski, a reporter for the *Los Angeles Times,* described the change that overcame the people of Baghdad to *Online NewsHour:*

> At first they were afraid to see the marines in their city and some of them even ran away. But they started to put out their white handkerchiefs and their white scarves and slowly approached them and pretty soon they were shaking hands and hugging them. And I think it also was remarkable to see the changes on their face when they realized that indeed President Saddam Hussein was no more. They could speak their mind and the kind of fear that has lingered over their lives all these years was melting away.

Some areas of Baghdad erupted in celebrations to mark the end of Hussein's rule. Many people waved and cheered at passing coalition troops and tore down posters of Hussein. One of the largest celebrations took place in Firdos Square in the center of Baghdad, where a large statue of Hussein stood. A group of Iraqi men climbed up the statue, attached ropes to its head, and tried to pull it down. When U.S. Marines came upon this scene, they used an armored vehicle to help the men topple the statue. The large crowd broke the statue into pieces and dragged its head through the streets. They also pounded the fallen statue with their shoes, which is considered a serious insult in the Arab world.

Footage of this scene appeared on television and in newspapers around the world. The toppling of the statue came to symbolize the fall of Hussein's regime. "It is a great

feeling," said one of the participants, twenty-year-old Iraqi student Ayass Mohammed, in *War on Saddam.* "I have never felt this way before. It was only two hours ago when suddenly I feel freedom, when I saw the American tanks and heard that the regime had run. All my life all I know is Saddam. Now we are free."

As the coalition forces took control of the Iraqi capital, members of Hussein's government fled the city. Sahaf, the information minister, simply did not show up for work on April 9. Neither did the official government "minders" who usually accompanied foreign journalists in Baghdad, setting strict limits on where they could go and whom they could talk to. As a result, many reporters suddenly found themselves with uncensored access to the city.

A crowd of Iraqis pull down a statue of Saddam Hussein in Baghdad after U.S. troops captured the capital city. The pulling down of the statue symbolized the end of Saddam Hussein's rule in Iraq. *Photograph by Scott Nelson. Getty Images. Reproduced by permission.*

Looting, resistance fighters cause problems

While celebrations took place in some parts of Baghdad, the reaction was mixed in other parts of the city. Although most Iraqis were glad to be rid of Hussein, many were suspicious of U.S. motives for invading Iraq. Some believed that the U.S. government wanted to control Iraq to take its oil. They also worried that Hussein or someone like him would return to power as soon as the American troops left Iraq. Finally, some expressed frustration about continued shortages of food, water, and medicine. They had hoped that humanitarian aid would become available more quickly.

Although the fall of Baghdad provided the coalition troops with a morale boost, they soon learned how much work still had to be done to secure the city. On the campus of Baghdad University, 2 miles (3.2 kilometers) away from the toppled statue in Firdos Square, U.S. Marines came under heavy fire from resistance fighters. Coalition troops also began to see looting and unrest all over the city. Iraqis who had suffered many years of hardship under Hussein's government began breaking into government buildings and private homes and carrying off everything of value they could find, including furniture, lights, computers, and air conditioners. They stole drugs and medical equipment from hospitals and looted the Iraqi National Museum for antiquities (valuable artifacts from ancient civilizations). The Bush administration drew heavy criticism for failing to anticipate this possibility. The coalition troops worked hard to restore order and clean up the damage. They also tried to identify centers of resistance and either defeat them or persuade them to surrender.

Fighting continues in northern Iraq

The fall of Baghdad did not mark the end of the Iraq War. Fighting continued for several more days in the northern part of Iraq. On April 10 coalition forces, including Kurdish *peshmerga* (meaning "those who face death") opposition fighters, moved into the city of Kirkuk. The coalition troops received their most enthusiastic welcome when they took over this northern city, which was home to many people of Kurdish descent. A short time later the Iraqi army surrendered in Mosul, leaving Hussein's hometown of Tikrit as the last major city not under coalition control. Many military experts expected coalition forces to face intense resistance in Tikrit. After all, the city had done well under Hussein's regime and was home to many of his relatives and most loyal supporters.

As the coalition troops moved toward Tikrit, they received a pleasant surprise. An Iraqi policeman tipped them off to the location of the seven remaining U.S. prisoners of war. The POWs included the five surviving members of Lynch's maintenance company and two crew members from an Apache helicopter that was shot down on March 24. They were being held in a prison in Samarra, about 40 miles (64 kilometers) north of Baghdad. The prison guards left their posts as the coalition troops approached, and one of them told U.S. military leaders about the prisoners. The POWs were reclaimed in a hastily arranged rescue mission.

During the battle for Tikrit on April 13, the coalition once again faced less resistance than expected. They soon took control of the city and captured several important members of Hussein's government, including his half brother Barzan Ibrahim Hasan al-Tikriti. Tikriti had served Hussein in several roles, including that of personal banker. After Tikrit fell to coalition forces, U.S. Army General Tommy Franks (1945–) declared an end to Hussein's rule in Iraq. "The Iraqi army has been destroyed," he said, as quoted in *War on Saddam.* "There's no regime command and control in existence right now. This is an ex-regime."

U.S. Army General Tommy Franks declared an end to Saddam Hussein's rule after Hussein's hometown of Tikrit fell to coalition forces. *Photograph by Scott Martin. AP/Wide World Photos. Reproduced by permission.*

At a Pentagon briefing the following day, Major General Stanley McChrystal told reporters that major combat operations in Iraq were over. Although he admitted that some resistance remained, he declared that Saddam Hussein was no longer in power. He indicated that the war was entering a phase of smaller, sharper fights to dislodge pockets of resistance. The major combat operations claimed the lives of 126 American soldiers (less than half as many as were killed during the 1991 Persian Gulf War) and wounded 495 others. The Arab television network Abu Dhabi reported that 1,250 Iraqi civilians had been killed and another 5,100 wounded in the fighting, but other sources estimated the totals to be much higher.

Bush announces end of major combat operations

On April 15 the coalition held a meeting of Iraqi opposition leaders in the ancient town of Ur in southern Iraq. The purpose of the meeting was to discuss Iraq's future government. The meeting included representatives of the Shiite Muslims of southern Iraq and the Kurds of northern Iraq. Both of these groups had suffered under Hussein's Sunni Muslim government. Since Hussein did not allow any political opposition, many people who attended the meeting had been living in exile outside Iraq for many years. They all hoped to have a say in the country's future.

Over the next two weeks, the U.S.-led coalition continued to target pockets of resistance. Many parts of Iraq remained dangerous, and small clashes took place throughout the country. But the coalition's main mission involved keeping order in Iraq's cities, securing its oil fields, protecting its antiquities, and searching for weapons of mass destruction. The troops also continued locating and capturing former members of Hussein's government. Every U.S. and British soldier received a special deck of playing cards to help them identify the fifty-five most wanted members of the regime. Each card featured a picture of an Iraqi official, along with his name and rank in Hussein's government. Hussein himself was the "ace of spades," or the highest card in the deck.

One well-known member of Hussein's government surrendered to U.S. authorities in Baghdad on April 24. Tariq Aziz (1936–) had acted as the Iraqi information minister during the 1991 Persian Gulf War and was widely considered the face of the regime by the outside world. His card was the eight of spades, making him number forty-three on the list of the fifty-five most wanted officials.

"Mission accomplished"

On April 30 U.S. Secretary of Defense Donald Rumsfeld (1932–) visited Baghdad to view rebuilding efforts and

Every U.S. and British soldier received a special deck of playing cards, like the one pictured here, to help them identify the fifty-five most wanted members of Saddam Hussein's regime. *©Reuters NewMedia Inc./Corbis. Reproduced by permission.*

meet with coalition leaders. The following day President Bush made a historic speech in which he declared that major combat operations in Iraq were over after forty-three days of fighting. The president chose to make the announcement in a dramatic fashion from the flight deck of the aircraft carrier USS *Abraham Lincoln*. The ship had been stationed in the Persian Gulf, but it was sailing off the coast of California at the time of the speech. Bush was flown to the ship in the copilot's seat of a U.S. Navy S-3B Viking jet. He wore a flight suit that indicated his military rank as commander in chief. The bridge of the ship was decorated with a large banner reading "Mission Accomplished."

In his speech, Bush praised the performance of U.S. and coalition troops in Iraq. "My fellow Americans, major combat operations in Iraq have ended. In the battle of Iraq, the United States and our allies have prevailed [won]," he said, as quoted by *CNN.com*. "Operation Iraqi Freedom was carried out with a combination of precision and speed and boldness the enemy did not expect and the world had not seen before."

Bush congratulated the coalition troops for bringing freedom to the Iraqi people. He acknowledged that they still had work to do: capture leaders of the former regime, locate hidden weapons, and reconstruct the country. But he claimed that the successful war effort was an important step in the war against terrorism. "The liberation of Iraq is a crucial advance in the campaign against terror," he stated. "We have removed an ally of Al Qaeda [a radical Islamic terrorist group responsible for the September 11, 2001, terrorist attacks against the United States] and cut off a source of terrorist funding."

Following the speech, analysts noted that Bush did not formally declare the Iraq War to be over. Instead, he announced an end to "major combat operations." They believed the president did this intentionally to keep his options open. Under international law, declaring the war to be over could complicate the coalition's efforts to track down former members of Hussein's regime. Coalition forces were still questioning thousands of Iraqi prisoners of war, and declaring an end to the war would have required those prisoners to be released.

Although many Americans found Bush's speech stirring, others criticized what came to be known as the "aircraft carrier speech." Some critics suggested that Bush had staged the speech to increase his own popularity and political power. They pointed out that the *Lincoln*, which was on its way home after ten months in the Persian Gulf, had been turned around and sent back out to sea so that the U.S. coastline would not be visible to TV cameras. They also complained about Bush's decision to be flown to the ship on a fighter jet. Although it provided dramatic news footage, the flight creat-

ed a security risk for Bush and cost American taxpayers a considerable amount of money. Pointing out that the *Lincoln* was well within helicopter range of the U.S. Naval Base in San Diego, California, Democratic Senator Robert Byrd (1917–) condemned Bush's "flamboyant showmanship" and called it "an affront [insult] to the Americans killed or injured in Iraq." Some critics also resented the fact that Bush presented himself as a military man when he had used his family connections to secure a post in the Texas Air National Guard and avoid active duty during the Vietnam War (1955–75).

Finally, some people felt it was too early to announce the end of combat operations in Iraq. They questioned whether the U.S. military had really accomplished its mission. After all, Hussein and his sons had escaped, no evidence of weapons of mass destruction had been found, and no concrete plans for Iraq's future existed. Some analysts believed that reconstructing Iraq and forming a democratic government would be the most difficult tasks of all.

Crew members aboard the USS *Lincoln* where President Bush gave what has become known as the "aircraft carrier speech" announcing the end of major combat in Iraq. *Photograph by Joe Raedle. Getty Images. Reproduced by permission.*

Building a Democratic Iraq 12

T he U.S.-led military campaign known as Operation Iraqi Freedom succeeded in removing Iraqi President Saddam Hussein (1937–) from power after only six weeks of fighting. In addition to ending a brutal regime and bringing the prospect of freedom to the people of Iraq, the war demonstrated the strength and technological superiority of the American military. As soon as the war ended, the Bush administration began working to rebuild Iraq and help its people create a democratic government (a form of government in which the people govern the country through elected representatives).

But Bush's postwar plans soon ran into trouble. Security became a concern as Iraqi insurgents (people who fight against an established government or occupation force) and foreign fighters launched a series of violent attacks against American troops and international aid workers in Iraq. The lack of security made it difficult for humanitarian aid to reach the Iraqi people, so the poor conditions in the country were slow to improve. Despite massive searches, no evidence of weapons of mass destruction was found in Iraq, which raised questions about the Bush administration's stated reasons for going to war. The United States and the United Nations (UN) argued over who should take responsibility for rebuilding Iraq and overseeing its transition to democracy.

Overall, some progress was made toward creating a new Iraqi government and rebuilding important facilities in the war-torn country. But by the end of 2003, some analysts wondered whether the conflict may have actually decreased America's national security, rather than making America safer, as the Bush administration claimed, by straining its relations with its longtime allies and creating more anti-U.S. feelings in the Arab world.

Experts praise the coalition's military performance

The one element of the Iraq War that received widespread approval was the performance of U.S. and coalition troops. The conduct of the war received a great deal of praise from military analysts. Retired U.S. Air Force Major General Don Sheppard, who commented on the Iraq War for *CNN.com,* called it "a textbook case for the war colleges for the future."

The U.S. strategy used a relatively small number of ground forces and focused on speed and flexibility. It relied on intelligence (information gathered through spying) to locate Iraqi government and military targets, and then used precision-guided "smart" bombs to destroy the targets, ideally without damaging nearby civilian (nonmilitary) facilities. "It was in some ways a new kind of war, swift in its execution, light and flexible in its tactics, making strategic use of Special Operations forces, real-time intelligence, and precision targeting," Todd Purdum wrote in *A Time of Our Choosing.* The U.S. war plan and state-of-the-art military technology allowed coalition forces to advance quickly toward Baghdad, easily overcoming the limited Iraqi resistance.

During the 1991 Persian Gulf War, only 9 percent of coalition bombs were precision-guided. That number increased to 70 percent during the 2003 Iraq War, according to Purdum. Many analysts credited the coalition's easy victory to its ability to identify and hit targets, day or night, in any kind of weather. The use of "smart" bombs also prevented large-scale civilian deaths and limited the damage to Iraq's infrastructure (roads, bridges, buildings, oil facilities, and so on). "What's happened is amazing for the speed with which it was executed, but also for all the things that did not happen, all the bad things that could have happened, because of that speed," said U.S. Secretary of Defense Donald Rumsfeld (1932–), as quoted by *CNN.com*. After the war ended, however, some people wondered whether the coalition's rapid military success contributed to the problems that plagued the reconstruction effort.

Reconstruction plans run into trouble

Bush administration officials outlined their plans for the reconstruction of Iraq even before the war ended. The original plans required U.S. troops to maintain security, oversee the rebuilding of Iraq's infrastructure, distribute aid to the Iraqi people, create an interim (temporary) government, and supervise the transition to a democratic government. "We have to help Iraqis restore their basic services," Rumsfeld explained, as quoted in *Online NewsHour*. "And we have to help provide conditions of stability and security so that the Iraqi people can form an interim authority, an interim government, and then ultimately a free Iraqi government based on political freedom, individual liberty, and the rule of law."

Retired U.S. Army General Jay Garner (1938–) was placed in charge of the reconstruction effort in January 2003. He was replaced in May by former diplomat and U.S. State Department official L. Paul Bremer III (1941–). Bremer became head of the Coalition Provisional Authority, a civil administration that still reported to the U.S. secretary of defense. The handover from Garner to Bremer symbolized

In May 2003 L. Paul Bremer III became the head of the Coalition Provisional Authority, a civil administration charged with the reconstruction effort in Iraq. *AP/Wide World Photos, Inc. Reproduced by permission.*

Iraq's transition from military to civilian authority following the end of combat operations. At around the same time, the U.S. military presence in Iraq was placed under the command of Lieutenant General John Abizaid (1951–), a Lebanese American who could speak Arabic.

The Bush administration's original reconstruction plans were based on their belief that the Iraqi people would welcome coalition troops as "liberators" who freed them from Hussein's brutal regime, rather than viewing them as foreign invaders. They believed that military success in Iraq would create pro-American feelings among the Iraqi people and encourage them to work toward establishing a democratic government and a new economy. But the coalition forces were rarely greeted by cheering crowds. Instead, most Iraqis either resented the presence of foreign soldiers in their country or worried that Hussein would return to power as soon as the troops left. Some Iraqi civilians put up fierce resistance against the coalition troops.

The administration also counted on the use of precision-guided weapons to limit the damage to Iraq's infrastructure and oil fields and thus make reconstruction easier. In fact, these facilities did not suffer much damage during the 2003 war. But many industrial plants were in bad shape due to neglect and a lack of maintenance during the decade of UN economic sanctions against Iraq. (Economic sanctions are trade restrictions intended to punish a country for breaking international law.) Other facilities were damaged by Iraqis during and after the war through looting, vandalism, and sabotage, such as destroying oil and water pipelines. These factors complicated the reconstruction effort and made the cost of rebuilding much higher.

Administration officials knew that Hussein's fall would create a power vacuum in Iraq, so they expected some security problems during the postwar period. But the situation in Iraq turned out to be much different and more complicated than they thought. Shortly after Baghdad fell to coalition forces, widespread looting and violence broke out across the city. Some Iraqis broke into Hussein's palaces and stole everything of value they could find. Angry mobs gathered outside government buildings and set several on fire, including the Information Ministry. Some people used the chaos as an opportunity to take revenge on their enemies.

Troops struggle to maintain security

Many observers felt that the coalition forces should have done more to maintain order in Baghdad. But the troops' rapid advance to the capital meant that there were not enough soldiers to provide effective security. In addition, the forces that occupied the city were not trained as peacekeepers. To complicate the situation, one of Bremer's first acts as head of the Coalition Provisional Authority was to disband Iraq's army and security forces. He did this because he was worried that Iraqi civilians would not trust people who had worked for Hussein to enforce the new rule of law. When unrest broke out in Baghdad and other cities, however, some observers questioned Bremer's decision. Critics claimed that a trained Iraqi security force could have prevented much of the violence. Others worried about what problems the now-unemployed soldiers' bitterness toward the U.S. leaders might cause.

As it turned out, the lack of effective security in the days following the end of the war did lasting damage to the Americans' image among the Iraqi people. "Frankly, the people are beginning to lose their trust in America," declared Walid al-Fartousi, a Baghdad fruit and vegetable vendor, in *A Time of Our Choosing.* "Because America promised Iraq to remove the tyrant government, but now things are even worse. Some people are even beginning to wish Saddam had stayed because all the troubles erupted after his departure.... There is no security, no order. People do not feel safe." Still, Bush administration officials believed that the situation would improve with time. "You cannot do everything instantaneously [all at once]," Rumsfeld argued in *A Time of Our Choosing.* "Freedom's untidy. And free people are free to make mistakes and commit crimes and do bad things. They're also free to live their lives and do wonderful things."

The UN seeks a larger role in reconstruction

As the weeks passed following the end of combat operations, the confusion and disorder continued in many parts of Iraq. The Bush administration's reconstruction plans came under increasingly harsh criticism in Iraq, in the United States, and internationally. Critics claimed that U.S. leaders had failed to set out a clear and complete plan for Iraq's reconstruction. They wanted American officials to set a concrete timetable for Iraq to achieve its independence and for U.S. troops to withdraw. But the Bush administration resisted calls for a firm deadline. Bush said at one point that U.S. forces would occupy Iraq for "as long as it takes."

Some critics claimed that the slow transition from combat to nation building in Iraq threatened to turn a major military victory into a political, economic, and humanitarian disaster. "Today we're at the high point of our military credibility but sadly, we're at the low point of our political credibility," said Zbigniew Brzezinski (1928–), former national security adviser to President Jimmy Carter (1924–; served 1977–81) and an analyst for *Online NewsHour*. "Very few people in the world really feel comfortable with the way we did it [conquered Iraq], particularly internationally, and very few people are convinced we'll exploit [use] the victory to translate the military success into an enduring political success."

The United Nations pressed President Bush to give the international community a larger role in the reconstruction of Iraq. The UN especially wanted to help shape the new Iraqi government. UN leaders warned that the international community's approval was needed to establish the legitimacy of the new administration in Iraq. "The military can bring about an absence of war, but what is going to be required are civilian agencies, the international community to bring about the peace," explained retired U.S. Army General George Joulwan, a former supreme allied commander of North Atlantic Treaty Organization (NATO) forces and an analyst for *Online NewsHour*. (NATO is an alliance of nineteen countries, including the United States, that have agreed to defend one another in wartime.) "We not only have to win the war, we have got to win the peace. That is going to take a concerted [intense] effort and that's going to take time."

But U.S. leaders were determined to maintain their control over reconstruction. Bush wanted the UN to play a role in providing food, medicine, and humanitarian aid to the people of Iraq, but he insisted that the United States would handle Iraq's political transition alone.

On May 22 the UN Security Council passed Resolution 1483, which recognized the United States and Great Britain as "occupying powers" in Iraq. This status gave the

U.S. soldiers patrol the streets in a suburb of Baghdad after clashes with Iraqi resistance fighters. Coalition forces continued to face dangerous situations in Iraq even after the major combat had been declared over. *Patrick Baz/AFP/Getty Images. Reproduced by permission.*

two countries specific obligations under international law, such as the responsibility to protect the civilian population in the occupied country. The resolution also outlined a series of initial steps with regard to UN participation in the reconstruction process. For example, it lifted the economic sanctions that had affected Iraq for more than ten years; appointed a UN special representative, longtime diplomat Sergio Vieira de Mello (1948–2003), to speak for the UN in Baghdad;

and set up a billion-dollar development fund for humanitarian and reconstruction needs in Iraq. "Whatever view each of us may take of the events of recent months, it is vital to all of us that the outcome is a stable democratic Iraq at peace with itself and with its neighbors, and contributing to the stability of the region," UN Secretary-General Kofi Annan (1938–) told *Online NewsHour.*

But the UN resolution caused problems in Iraq. Some Iraqis were angry that the U.S. military presence in Iraq had been officially designated as an "occupation" (the control of a country by a foreign military force). This led some Iraqis to doubt Bush's claim that the United States had no interest in taking over Iraq. Many Iraqis reacted to the resolution by demanding that the United States move more quickly to transfer political power back to the Iraqi people.

Coalition troops encounter growing resistance

The attacks against coalition forces in Iraq began to increase in June, to an average of about two dozen per day. The Iraqi resistance movement seemed to become more determined and organized as time went on. It included former members of Hussein's Baath Party government, as well as foreign fighters from nearby countries, such as Syria, Iran, and Yemen. Some of the insurgents were Islamic extremists with ties to Al Qaeda and other international terrorist organizations. (Al Qaeda is a radical Islamic terrorist group responsible for the September 11, 2001, terrorist attacks against the United States.) They hated the U.S. occupation of a Muslim country and targeted coalition forces as well as Iraqi citizens who appeared to be cooperating with the coalition.

The resistance movement appeared to have several different goals. Some fighters simply wanted to force the coalition troops to leave Iraq. They believed that if they could inflict enough casualties (dead and wounded soldiers), the American people would demand that Bush withdraw his troops. "Failing to win the conventional war, they began an unconventional war focused on dueling civilizations," wrote Williamson Murray and Robert H. Scales Jr. in *The Iraq War: A Military History.* "If they could kill enough Americans in the name of religion and culture, then perhaps they would regain the support of the Iraqi people and others in the Islamic world, and the Americans would become discouraged by the human cost and withdraw."

Other insurgents fought to preserve the influence of Islamic law and Arab culture in Iraq. Even the leaders of some nearby countries felt threatened by the prospect of a secular (nonreligious), democratic government in the heart of the Middle East. "Iraq is the nexus [center] where many issues are coming together—Islam versus democracy, the West versus the axis of evil, Arab nationalism versus some different types of political culture," Barham Saleh, a Kurdish official in northern Iraq, said in *A Time of Our Choosing*. "If the Americans succeed here, this will be a monumental [huge] blow to everything the terrorists stand for."

The violent resistance created a tense and dangerous situation for coalition forces in Iraq. But Bush remained determined. He warned the insurgents that their actions would not persuade him to withdraw American troops. In one controversial statement, he seemed to issue a challenge to the attackers. "There are some who feel like if they attack us that we may decide to leave prematurely [too early]," he said in early July, according to *A Time of Our Choosing*. "They don't understand what they're talking about, if that's the case.... My answer is, bring 'em on." Many people criticized the phrase "bring 'em on," saying that it seemed to be daring the insurgents to kill U.S. soldiers. But others felt it was simply an expression of confidence in U.S. troops.

Search fails to uncover weapons of mass destruction

After reaching an all-time high of 70 percent in April 2003, Bush's approval ratings began to fall in July. The continuing attacks on coalition troops contributed to the decline, as did concerns that the Bush administration did not have a clear plan for the reconstruction of Iraq. At the time, the White House was also facing a scandal concerning its reasons for launching the war against Iraq.

On July 6, 2003, the *New York Times* published an article accusing the Bush administration of exaggerating

Iraqi Opposition Groups

The major political figures in the new Iraqi government come from the many opposition groups that resisted Saddam Hussein's rule. Although dozens of opposition groups existed both within and outside Iraq, a handful emerged as the most powerful. In the years leading up to the 2003 Iraq War, U.S. leaders provided support to some of these groups. They hoped that the Iraqi opposition might organize a successful uprising that would remove Hussein from power, thus avoiding a direct U.S. military invasion. U.S. government officials also consulted with the leaders of these groups to identify the weaknesses in Hussein's defenses and measure the level of popular support for an invasion among the Iraqi people. But the main Iraqi opposition groups differed greatly in their membership and goals, which raised questions about their ability to cooperate and form a democratic government in Iraq.

Two of the strongest opposition groups formed among the non-Arab Kurds of northern Iraq. The Kurdistan Democratic Party (KDP) controls the northwestern part of the autonomous (self-governed) region known as Iraqi Kurdistan. The Patriotic Union of Kurdistan (PUK) controls the southeastern part of Iraqi Kurdistan. Both of these groups have a long history of resistance to Iraq's central government and have played a significant role in Iraqi politics. Their main goal is to break off from Iraq and form an independent Kurdish nation. Since their membership is based on tribal loyalty, the two groups have shared

an uneasy balance of power over the years. The Kurdish independence movement in Iraq also faces resistance from the governments of nearby Turkey and Iran, which want to prevent their own Kurdish populations from declaring independence.

Founded in 1946, the KDP is led by Kurdish tribal leader Massoud Barzani (1946–). KDP fighters sided with Iran during the Iran-Iraq War (1980–88). Hussein's army responded by arresting thousands of members of the Barzani clan, most of whom were never seen again. Following the 1991 Persian Gulf War, the KDP took part in the widespread Iraqi uprisings against Hussein's government. When the expected U.S. military support failed to materialize, Hussein's army crushed the uprising and two million Kurds were forced to flee across the mountains into Turkey and Iran. Many Kurds felt betrayed by the United States, which made them reluctant to support the 2003 U.S. invasion of Iraq. Ultimately, however, Kurdish fighters helped American forces capture several cities in northern Iraq.

Founded in the nearby country of Syria in 1975, the PUK is led by Jalal Talabani (1933–). This group also supported Iran during the Iran-Iraq War. Hussein's regime responded in 1988 with the "Anfal" campaign, in which the Iraqi army used poison gas to destroy thousands of Kurdish villages and kill more than five thousand Kurds. PUK fighters were forced to flee to Iran, but they returned to take part in the 1991 uprisings against Hussein's government. In 1996 tensions between the two Kurdish political groups erupted into a civil war, and the KDP accepted assistance from the Iraqi army to push back the PUK. A peace agreement brokered by the United States favored the KDP, but relations between the two groups have remained peaceful since then.

Another leading Iraqi opposition group is the Iraqi National Accord. Founded in 1990 with the support of Saudi Arabia, it is composed largely of former military and security officials in Hussein's government who left Iraq. Most of its members are Sunni Muslims. Its leader, Iyad Alawi, was a senior Iraqi intelligence officer who left Iraq in 1971. The Iraqi National Accord's main strategy involved attracting dissatisfied military and security officers within Iraq and trying to organize an overthrow of Hussein's government. In 1996 it organized a disastrous military coup against Hussein. Hussein's security force uncovered the plot and captured and executed the one hundred officers involved. Before the 2003 Iraq War, the Iraqi National Accord used its contacts among Iraqi military and security forces to encourage them not to fight.

The main religious group to oppose Hussein's rule was the Supreme Council for the Islamic Revolution in Iraq (SCIRI). Founded in 1982 in Iran, its aim is to protect the country's Islamic spiritual identity and values. Its membership consists mainly of Iraqi Shiite exiles. It has been criticized over the years for its close ties to Iran, which U.S. leaders view as a dangerous, unfriendly nation. The SCIRI organized some of the Shiite uprisings that took control of several major cities in southern Iraq following the 1991 Persian Gulf War. Hussein's army crushed the uprisings when the rebels failed to gain U.S. military support. Many Shiite leaders were executed, and a number of villages and mosques (religious temples) were destroyed. Despite his distrust of the U.S. government, the SCIRI's leader, Ayatollah Muhammad Bakar Al-Hakim, cooperated with the 2003 invasion. He was killed shortly after the war ended when a car bomb destroyed a mosque near Najaf. He was succeeded by his brother, Abdul Aziz al-Hakim.

Another influential opposition group is the Iraqi National Congress (INC), led by Iraqi exile Ahmad Chalabi (1944–). Formed in 1992, the INC was originally intended to act as an umbrella organization for all of the major Iraqi opposition groups. A statement of its purpose, quoted in *The Iraq War Reader,* says that it "provides an institutional framework so that the popular will of the Iraqi people ... can be democratically determined and implemented [put into practice]." At one time the INC had 234 members representing 90 percent of the Iraqi opposition groups. In the mid-1990s it lost some influence due to infighting between the Kurdish groups, and it ended up relocating its headquarters from northern Iraq to London. The INC has been criticized over the years for its close ties to the United States and its lack of popular support among the people of Iraq.

Sources: What Lies Beneath. *Washington, DC: International Crisis Group, 2002;* "A Who's Who of the Iraqi Opposition." *In Sifry, Micah L., and Christopher Serf, eds.* The Iraq War Reader. *New York: Simon and Schuster, 2003.*

the threat posed by Hussein and his alleged weapons of mass destruction. Joseph Wilson (1959–), a former U.S. ambassador to several countries in Africa, told the paper that the Central Intelligence Agency (CIA) had sent him to Africa to find out whether Iraq had tried to purchase uranium (a rare, radioactive element used in the construction of nuclear weapons) from Niger, a country in northern central Africa. Wilson checked out the story and determined that it was untrue. Upon returning to the United States in March 2002, he reported his findings to the CIA. Months later, however, President Bush included the accusation in his 2003 State of the Union address. Bush claimed that Iraq had tried to acquire uranium from Africa, which he said proved that Hussein was intent on building nuclear weapons. U.S. leaders later cited the need to prevent Iraq from acquiring nuclear capability as a major reason for launching the 2003 Iraq War.

Wilson came forward at a time when concern about the postwar situation in Iraq was increasing. He claimed that the Bush administration knowingly misused intelligence information to make its case for going to war. "Based on my experience with the administration in the months leading up to the war, I have little choice but to conclude that some of the intelligence related to Iraq's nuclear weapons program was twisted to exaggerate the Iraqi threat," Wilson stated, as quoted by *ABCNews.com.* Wilson's article proved a major embarrassment for the administration and increased doubts about the accuracy of the president's other claims regarding Iraq.

During the months following the end of combat operations, UN and U.S. inspectors conducted a massive search for weapons of mass destruction in Iraq. More than a thousand inspectors combed the country and interviewed former members of Hussein's regime, at a cost of hundreds of millions of dollars. By the end of 2003, they had not uncovered any evidence that Iraq possessed weapons of mass destruction. In fact, the evidence available suggested that Iraq's weapons programs had been discontinued in the mid-1990s.

If Iraq did not possess nuclear, chemical, or biological weapons, then it was unclear why Hussein refused to cooperate fully with UN weapons inspectors in the months leading

Members of the Iraq Governing Council

The first transitional government in Iraq following the fall of Saddam Hussein was called the Iraq Governing Council. Its membership included twenty-five leading Iraqis whose political, ethnic, and religious backgrounds reflected the diversity of Iraq's population. The original members of the council, and their religious and political affiliations, were:

Ahmad Chalabi (Shiite): Founder of the Iraqi National Congress.

Abdul Aziz al-Hakim (Shiite): Leader of the Supreme Council for the Islamic Revolution in Iraq.

Iyad Alawi (Shiite): Leader of the Iraqi National Accord.

Ibrahim al-Jafari (Shiite): Leader of the Daawa Islamic Party.

Abdel-Zahraa Othman Mohammed (Shiite): Member of the Daawa Islamic Party.

Hamid Majid Moussa (Shiite): Leader of the Communist Party.

Abdel-Karim Mahoud al-Mohammedawi (Shiite): Member of the Hezbollah Party.

Ahmed al-Barak (Shiite): Human rights activist.

Aquila al-Hashimi (Shiite): Foreign affairs expert and diplomat (assassinated in September 2003).

Raja Habib al-Khuzai (Shiite): Hospital director.

Mohammed Bahr al-Uloum (Shiite): Cleric from Najaf.

Wael Abdul Latif (Shiite): Judge and governor of Basra.

Mouwafak al-Rabii (Shiite): Doctor and human rights activist.

Adnan Pachachi (Sunni): Former foreign minister and Iraqi ambassador to the UN.

Nasir al-Chadirch (Sunni): Leader of the National Democratic Party.

Mohsen Abdel Hamid (Sunni): Leader of the Iraqi Islamic Party.

Ghazi Mashal Ajil al-Yawer (Sunni): Northern tribal leader.

Samir Shakir Mahmoud (Sunni): Writer.

Massoud Barzani (Sunni Kurd): Leader of the Kurdistan Democratic Party.

Jalal Talabani (Sunni Kurd): Leader of the Patriotic Union of Kurdistan.

Salaheddine Bahaaeddin (Sunni Kurd): Leader of the Kurdistan Islamic Union.

Mahmoud Othman (Sunni Kurd): Founder of the Kurdish Socialist Party.

Dara Noor Alzin (Sunni Kurd): Judge.

Younadem Kana (Assyrian Christian): Engineer and trade minister.

Sondul Chapouk (Turkoman): Engineer, teacher, and activist.

Sources: *"The Iraq Governing Council." Online NewsHour. Available online at* http://www.pbs.org/newshour/bb/middle_east/iraq/postwar/player_3.html *(accessed on January 8, 2004);* White, Thomas E., et al. Reconstructing Eden: A Comprehensive Plan for the Postwar Political and Economic Development of Iraq. *Houston, TX: CountryWatch, 2003.*

up to the 2003 Iraq War. Some analysts claimed that Hussein resisted the inspections in order to save face and maintain his standing in the Arab world. Others thought that he allowed the world to believe that he possessed weapons of mass destruction in an effort to prevent military action by the United States, or to maintain his fear-based rule over the Iraqi people.

In any case, evidence collected after the war suggested that Iraq did not possess such weapons. In January 2004 a respected independent organization called the Carnegie Endowment for International Peace published a report stating that Iraq had not posed a threat to United States or world security before the 2003 war, despite the Bush administration's claims. "There are no large stockpiles of weapons," the report's author, weapons expert Joseph Cirincione, told *CNN.com.* "There hasn't actually been a find of a single weapon, a single weapons agent, nothing like the programs that the administration believe existed." The report also claimed that the Bush administration put pressure on the CIA to agree with its views regarding the threat posed by Iraq.

Iraq forms a transitional government

One week after Wilson published his article in the *New York Times,* Iraq took the first step toward forming a new, democratic government. The Iraq Governing Council (IGC), an interim government composed of twenty-five leading Iraqis from a range of political, ethnic, and religious backgrounds, held its first official meeting on July 13. The Coalition Provisional Authority chose the members of the IGC to reflect Iraq's population. For example, Shiite Muslims account for 60 percent of Iraq's population, so they received thirteen seats on the council. The IGC also included five Sunni Muslims, five non-Arab Kurds, one Christian, and one Turkoman. Three of the council members were women.

Many members of the IGC were the leaders of various groups that had opposed Hussein's government. Since Hussein often used violence to silence his political opponents, some of the council members had fled Iraq and lived in exile abroad for many years. Some people worried that these exiles might have problems winning the respect of those who had remained in

Iraq and suffered under Hussein's rule. Others wondered whether the different religious beliefs and ethnic backgrounds of the council might cause internal conflicts that would prevent it from addressing the needs of the Iraqi people.

But the IGC showed its determination to be a positive force for change in Iraq during its first meeting. The group's first official act was to ban six national holidays that had been put in place under Hussein's rule. They declared that Iraq's new national holiday would be April 9, the date Baghdad fell to coalition forces. They also began sending diplomats to visit foreign governments, setting up a budget, and forming a war crimes court to try former members of Hussein's government.

Over the next several months, the IGC continued to work toward forming a democratic government in Iraq. It faced pressures from various groups that wanted to advance their own interests. For example, the Kurds of northern Iraq wanted to make sure that the new government recognized their desire for an independent homeland. The Sunnis of central Iraq wanted assurance that their needs would not be ignored by a government largely controlled by Shiites. Shiite religious leaders in the south wanted to ensure that Islamic law played an important role in the principles of the new government. These conflicting interests sometimes made it difficult for the IGC to perform its duties.

The next steps in the political process included selecting a transitional assembly of 250 members representing Iraq's provinces, drafting and approving a new constitution, and holding free elections. Coalition leaders set a goal of handing over power to a sovereign [independent] Iraqi government by July 1, 2004. But they realized that it would be difficult to transfer political power to the Iraqis if coalition troops could not control the instability and violence within the country.

A series of terrorist attacks hit Iraq

One week after the IGC held its first meeting, the coalition located and eliminated two of the most-wanted members of Hussein's regime. On July 22 coalition leaders announced that Hussein's two sons, Qusay and Uday, had been killed in a six-hour shoot-out with U.S. troops in Mosul, a town in northern Iraq. Qusay (1966–2003) organized Hussein's brutal security force. He was chosen as the "ace of clubs," or second-highest card, in the special deck of playing cards issued to coalition troops to help them identify the fifty-five most-wanted members of the regime. Uday (1964–2003) was known for torturing and killing people in violent rampages. He was represented by the "ace of hearts," or third-highest card in the deck. Coalition forces were tipped off to the brothers' location by the owner of the house where they were staying. U.S. leaders had previously offered a $30 million reward for the two brothers. They positively identified the pair through dental records.

The Bush administration reacted to the news of Qusay and Uday's deaths with satisfaction and relief. They hoped that this evidence of Hussein's fall from power might persuade Baath Party loyalists to end their resistance. They even released photos and videotapes of the bodies in an effort to convince Iraqis that Hussein's sons were truly dead. But the attacks against coalition forces continued and even showed signs of greater coordination.

The first organized terrorist attack in Iraq took place on August 7, when a car bomb exploded outside the Jordanian embassy in Baghdad. Seventeen Iraqi civilians (people not involved in a war, including women and children) were killed in the attack. International terrorism experts pointed out that the attack took place on the anniversary of the date when U.S. troops were first sent to Saudi Arabia in response to Iraq's invasion of Kuwait in 1990. The Muslim cleric (religious leader) Osama bin Laden (1957–), who organized the September 11, 2001, terrorist attacks on the United States, cited the presence of American military forces in Saudi Arabia as a major motive for his actions. (Saudi Arabia is home to the sacred Muslim sites of Mecca and Medina, where millions of Islamic pilgrims travel every year. Bin Laden and many other Muslims, viewed the presence of foreign troops in the Islamic holy land as an offense to their religious beliefs.) The timing of the attack raised concerns that international terrorist groups were becoming involved in the violence in Iraq.

A second terrorist attack struck Baghdad on August 19, when a truck bomb destroyed much of the UN headquarters in Baghdad. The blast killed the UN's special representative to

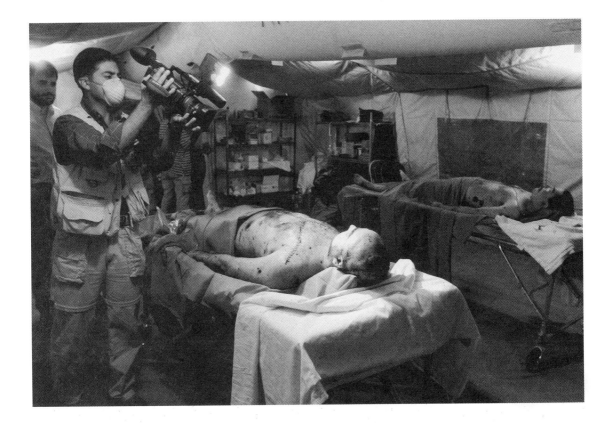

Iraq, Sergio Vieira de Mello, and twenty-two other people. At least one hundred more were wounded. Terrorism experts believed that this attack was intended to frighten civilian aid workers in Iraq. In response, the United Nations increased its security and pulled many of its staff out of Iraq. Other aid organizations followed its example and reduced their presence in Baghdad. Ten days later a car bomb destroyed the Imam Ali Mosque in Najaf, which Shiite Muslims considered the holiest shrine in Iraq. Nearly one hundred people were killed, including Ayatollah Muhammad Bakar al-Hakim (1939–2003), the most prominent Shiite religious leader who was cooperating with the coalition's reconstruction efforts.

Postwar costs rise

The continuing violence in Iraq took the lives of many American soldiers as well. A total of 138 U.S. soldiers had been killed from the beginning of the Iraq War to the time that

Cameramen film the bodies said to be those of Uday (left) and Qusay (right), sons of former Iraqi President Saddam Hussein. U.S. forces announced that Uday and Qusay were killed in a fierce gun battle in the northern Iraqi city of Mosul. *©Reuters NewMedia Inc./Corbis. Reproduced by permission.*

President Bush declared an end to combat operations on May 1. By the end of August, however, more U.S. troops had died in Iraq after the war ended than during the war itself. The number of postwar deaths topped 200 by the end of 2003. By January 2004 the total number of American soldiers killed in Iraq during and after the war had reached 500, making it the costliest U.S. military action since the Vietnam War (1955–75).

The continuing loss of American lives angered many U.S. citizens. Critics questioned Bush's control of the situation in Iraq and wondered whether the war was worth the cost. Three months after combat operations ended, 140,000 U.S. troops remained in Iraq. In contrast, there were only about 21,000 troops from other countries, and 11,000 of these were British. This meant that the other coalition partners had committed an average of fewer than 600 soldiers each. With large forces stationed in both Iraq and Afghanistan, the U.S. military was stretched thin. Some people were worried that the country would not be prepared to respond if a conflict broke out in another part of the world.

In addition to the cost in American lives, there was the high financial cost of postwar reconstruction. A report published by the World Bank and the United Nations estimated that the reconstruction of Iraq would cost $36 billion over four years. The Coalition Provisional Authority increased this estimate by $19 billion. Some Americans felt that the Bush administration should give up some control in Iraq to the United Nations so that other countries would contribute more money and commit more troops.

But President Bush resisted the idea of sharing power with the United Nations. He particularly disliked the idea of granting profitable postwar rebuilding contracts to companies from countries (such as France) that had opposed the war. Many of the early reconstruction contracts went to U.S. companies that had political ties to the Bush administration. For example, the energy company Halliburton, which was formerly headed by Vice President Dick Cheney (1941–), received a huge contract without having to bid for the job against other companies. Critics complained that such deals unfairly limited competition and made it more difficult to persuade other countries to contribute to rebuilding costs.

Request for $87 billion causes controversy

On September 7 Bush asked the U.S. Congress to approve a request for $87 billion to fund military operations and reconstruction work in Iraq and Afghanistan. Before the war began, administration officials had repeatedly claimed that proceeds from Iraq's oil industry could pay for the nation's reconstruction. The figure met with controversy, both in Congress and among American citizens. Two weeks later, in the face of criticism over the high costs of rebuilding Iraq, Bush officially asked the international community for help. On September 23 he addressed the United Nations and asked world leaders to play a larger role in Iraq's reconstruction. He specifically mentioned a need for the United Nations to assist Iraq in developing a constitution, training civil servants, and conducting free elections.

In October the Bush administration announced it intended to speed up the transfer of power to Iraqis. In a major

A U.S. Army Bradley fighting vehicle moves into position near a burnt humvee following a rocket propelled grenade attack on American troops in August 2003. *Photograph by Scott Nelson. Getty Images. Reproduced by permission.*

victory for Shiite religious leaders, the administration agreed to allow the Iraqi people to choose a new government before drafting a constitution. Several leading Shiites had refused to cooperate because they believed that only an elected Iraqi government should have the power to create a constitution. Otherwise, they argued, the new government would not have the support of the Iraqi people. U.S. officials, on the other hand, wanted its handpicked interim government, the IGC, to draft the constitution. U.S. leaders were also reluctant to hold elections while terrorist attacks and unrest were still such a problem.

As part of the effort to transfer more responsibility for reconstruction to Iraqis, coalition troops trained more than twenty thousand Iraqis to act as a security force. This force replaced U.S. troops in guarding such important facilities as embassies, ministries, banks, humanitarian aid offices, and oil fields. The Iraqi security officers accepted a dangerous job. Since they were cooperating with the occupation forces and working to stabilize the country, they became a major target for insurgents and were regularly attacked with bombs and other weapons, killing and wounding many of them.

Coalition troops capture Saddam Hussein

The violence in Iraq continued throughout the fall of 2003. In late September a member of the IGC, Aquila al-Hashimi, died of wounds she suffered when her car was ambushed by gunmen. Coalition leaders were not safe from the violence either. Deputy U.S. Defense Secretary Paul Wolfowitz (1943–) visited Iraq in October and barely escaped a rocket attack that hit the Al Rasheed Hotel in Baghdad. Bremer was nearly killed in December when his convoy of vehicles was ambushed by insurgents outside the capital. In early November Baghdad was rocked by a series of coordinated bombing attacks. Four bombs exploded in less than an hour outside police stations and at the aid organization International Red Cross headquarters. Thirty-four Iraqis and one American were killed in the bombings.

On Thanksgiving Day, November 27, President Bush made a surprise visit to Baghdad, where he helped serve dinner to soldiers and raised the spirits of American forces. Coalition leaders received more good news two weeks before

A newsstand sells papers with front pages that report the capture of former Iraqi leader Saddam Hussein. *Photograph by Graeme Robertson. Getty Images. Reproduced by permission.*

Christmas, when former Iraqi President Saddam Hussein was captured. Responding to a tip from an informant, the Raider Brigade of the U.S. Army's Fourth Infantry Division searched a farm near the town of Adwar, about 10 miles (16 kilometers) from Hussein's hometown of Tikrit. They found Hussein hiding in an 8-foot- (2.5-meter-) deep "spider hole," concealed with dirt and bricks, outside a mud hut on the property. The former Iraqi leader, who was found with a pistol and $750,000 in cash, surrendered peacefully. He looked shaggy, with a ragged beard instead of his usual neatly trimmed mustache, and seemed confused. The coalition released pictures of Hussein taken during a medical exam and after he was cleaned up and shaved as proof of his capture.

Bremer announced the capture to the world in a press conference the following day. "Ladies and gentlemen, we got him," he stated, as quoted in *Time* magazine. "Iraq's future, your future, has never been more full of hope. The tyrant is a prisoner." Iraqi journalists attending the news conference

A map showing the "Sunni triangle," an area in central Iraq where the coalition faced the fiercest resistance. *Map by XNR Productions, Inc. Thomson Gale. Reproduced by permission.*

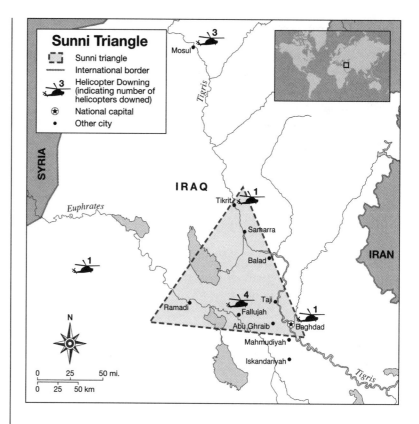

stood up and cheered or cried. Some screamed "Kill him! Kill Saddam!" When the people of Baghdad heard the news, some of them threw candy in the streets or fired guns into the sky in celebration. But others expressed sadness or anger at seeing the longtime leader of Iraq humiliated.

Bush was thrilled by the capture of Hussein, and he hoped it might persuade former regime members to end their resistance. But he also warned, "The capture of Saddam Hussein does not mean the end of violence in Iraq," according to the *Detroit Free Press.* "We still face terrorists who would rather go on killing the innocent than accept the rise of liberty in the heart of the Middle East." Interviews with Hussein following his capture yielded little evidence that he was involved in planning the attacks against coalition forces. Although some insurgents may have been motivated by a desire to see Hussein return to power, most seemed to be acting mainly out of hatred for the U.S. occupation of Iraq.

Iraq faces an uncertain future

The coalition rebuilding effort, led by the U.S. Agency for International Development (USAID), accomplished a great deal in Iraq by the end of 2003. For example, the agency rebuilt two thousand schools and vaccinated two million Iraqi children against diseases. Yet most Iraqis did not have better lives under coalition rule. Food and other goods were more readily available than before the war, thanks to the lifting of UN economic sanctions. But many Iraqis still did not have reliable electric power or safe drinking water, and severe gasoline shortages affected much of the country. When teams of reporters from ABC News and *Time* interviewed Iraqis six months after the end of the war, the majority said that overall living conditions were the same or worse than they had been under Saddam Hussein.

The second Persian Gulf War provided mixed results for President George W. Bush. *©Reuters NewMedia Inc./Corbis. Reproduced by permission.*

By the end of 2003, it remained to be seen whether the coalition would succeed in creating a stable, democratic government in Iraq. Although large parts of northern and southern Iraq were calm, ongoing violence made many people in central Iraq feel unsafe. The fiercest resistance took place within the "Sunni triangle," an area in central Iraq bordered by Baghdad in the east, the town of Ramadi in the west, and Hussein's hometown of Tikrit in the north. Coalition leaders believed that this area contained the largest number of Baath Party members and other Iraqis who remained loyal to Hussein.

One positive sign took place in late December 2003, when the Arab League sent its first official delegation to Iraq. (The Arab League is an alliance of twenty Arab nations and the Palestine Liberation Organization [PLO] that promotes political, military, and economic cooperation in the Arab world.) The Arab League had refused to work with the IGC up to this point because it believed the interim government was controlled by the United States. The official visit signaled an important change in attitude that could lead to better relations between Iraq and the rest of the Middle East. "Better late than never," IGC member Ibrahim al-Jafari told the *Christian Science Monitor.* "They've come to get to know us better and to be involved with the new Iraq. We have too many resources and too much cultural relevance to the Arab world to be ignored."

Iraq War provides mixed results for Bush

The Iraq War accomplished several important goals for the Bush administration. It removed a brutal dictator from power, ended decades of repression of the Iraqi people, and demonstrated the strength of the U.S. military. But it also cost the United States billions of dollars, committed its military to a long and uncertain process of nation building, and strained the alliances with other nations that the United States had depended on since World War II (1939–45).

The Bush administration claimed that it had entered the war in order to make Americans safer. Afterward, however, some analysts argued that the invasion of Iraq had caused widespread resentment in the Arab world and made it easier for terrorist groups to recruit new members. "There was every bit as much evidence—if not more—that the war had inflamed anti-American feeling in the Arab and Muslim lands and had put American lives and installations at fresh risk as there were signs that toppling Saddam had made America safer," Purdum wrote. A report published by the U.S. Army War College in December 2003 called the invasion of Iraq a "strategic error" that spread U.S. military forces too thin and distracted from the global war on terrorism.

But the Bush administration continued to express confidence that the Iraq War would improve both the lives of Iraqi citizens and America's long-term national security. They encouraged the American people to be patient with the reconstruction efforts. "You don't build democracy like you build a house," said Wolfowitz, as quoted in *A Time of Our Choosing.* "Democracy grows like a garden. If you keep the

weeds out and water the plants and you're patient, eventually you get something magnificent."

Where to Learn More

The following list focuses on works written for readers of middle school or high school age. Books aimed at adult readers have been included when they are especially important in providing information or analysis that would otherwise be unavailable.

Books

Al-Khalil, Samir. *Republic of Fear: The Inside Story of Saddam's Iraq.* Berkeley: University of California Press, 1989.

Al-Radi, Nuha. *Baghdad Diaries: A Woman's Chronicle of War and Exile.* New York: Vintage, 2003.

Alterman, Eric, and Mark J. Green. *The Book on Bush: How George W. (Mis)leads America.* New York: Viking, 2004.

Atkinson, Rick. *In the Company of Soldiers: A Chronicle of Combat.* New York: Holt, 2003.

Boyne, Walter J. *Operation Iraqi Freedom: What Went Right, What Went Wrong, and Why.* New York: Forge, 2003.

Cipkowski, Peter. *Understanding the Crisis in the Persian Gulf.* New York: John Wiley, 1992.

Cronkite, Walter. *LIFE: The War in Iraq.* New York: Time Life Books, 2003.

Editors of *Time* Magazine. *21 Days to Baghdad: Photos and Dispatches from the Battlefield.* New York: Time Life Books, 2003.

Foster, Leila M. *The Story of the Persian Gulf War.* Chicago: Children's Press, 1991.

Frum, David. *The Right Man: The Surprise Presidency of George W. Bush.* New York: Random House, 2003.

Garrels, Anne. *Naked in Baghdad: The Iraq War as Seen by NPR's Correspondent.* New York: Farrar, Straus, and Giroux, 2003.

Goldschmidt, Arthur. *A Concise History of the Middle East.* Boulder, CO: Westview Press, 1989.

Haskins, James. *Colin Powell: A Biography.* New York: Scholastic, 1992.

Katovsky, Bill, and Timothy Carlson. *Embedded: The Media at War in Iraq.* Guilford, CT: Lyons Press, 2003.

Kent, Zachary. *George Bush.* Chicago: Children's Press, 1993.

Kent, Zachary. *The Persian Gulf War: The Mother of All Battles.* Hillside, NJ: Enslow, 1994.

King, John. *The Gulf War.* New York: Dillon Press, 1991.

Lehr, Heather. *The Kurds.* Philadelphia: Chelsea House, 2003.

Miller, Judith, and Laurie Mylroie. *Saddam Hussein and the Crisis in the Gulf.* New York: Times Books, 1990.

Moore, Robin. *Hunting down Saddam: The Inside Story of the Search and Capture.* New York: St. Martin's, 2004.

NBC Enterprises. *Operation Iraqi Freedom: The Inside Story.* New York: NBC, 2003.

Pax, Salam. *Salam Pax: The Clandestine Diary of an Ordinary Iraqi.* New York: Grove Press, 2003.

Pimlott, John. *Middle East: A Background to the Conflicts.* New York: Franklin Watts, 1991.

Purdum, Todd S., and the staff of the *New York Times. A Time of Our Choosing: America's War in Iraq.* New York: Times Books, 2003.

Rai, Milan. *War Plan Iraq.* London: Verso, 2002.

Renfrew, Nita. *Saddam Hussein.* New York: Chelsea House, 1992.

Richie, Jason. *Iraq and the Fall of Saddam Hussein.* Minneapolis: Oliver Press, 2003.

Ridgeway, James. *The March to War.* New York: Four Walls Eight Windows, 1991.

Rivera, Sheila. *Operation Iraqi Freedom.* Edina, MN: Abdo, 2004.

Rivera, Sheila. *Rebuilding Iraq.* Edina, MN: Abdo, 2003.

Rooney, Ben. *The Daily Telegraph War on Saddam: The Complete Story of the Iraq Campaign.* London: Robinson, 2003.

Ryan, Mike. *Baghdad or Bust: The Inside Story of Gulf War II.* Yorkshire, UK: Leo Cooper, 2003.

Salzman, Marian, and Anne O'Reilly. *War and Peace in the Persian Gulf: What Teenagers Want to Know.* Princeton, NJ: Petersen's Guides, 1991.

Sasson, Jean P. *The Rape of Kuwait: The True Story of Iraq's Atrocities against a Civilian People.* New York: Knightsbridge, 1991.

Scheer, Christopher. *The Five Biggest Lies Bush Told about Iraq.* New York: Akashic Books, 2003.

Sciolino, Elaine. *The Outlaw State: Saddam Hussein's Quest for Power and the Gulf Crisis.* New York: John Wiley, 1991.

Sifry, Micah L., and Christopher Serf, eds. *The Iraq War Reader.* New York: Simon and Schuster, 2003.

Steloff, Rebecca. *Norman Schwarzkopf.* New York: Chelsea House, 1992.

White, Thomas E., et al. *Reconstructing Eden: A Comprehensive Plan for the Postwar Political and Economic Development of Iraq.* Houston: Country Watch, 2003.

Videos and DVDs

CNN Presents: The War in Iraq—The Road to Baghdad. Wea Corp, 2003.

National Geographic: 21 Days to Baghdad. Warner Home Video, 2003.

Nightline: War against Iraq Begins. Mpi Home Video, 2001.

21st Century Guide to Operation Iraqi Freedom. U.S. Department of Defense, 2003.

War in the Desert. Red Distribution, Inc., 2003.

Web Sites

"Fog of War." *Washington Post.* Available at http://www.washingtonpost.com/wp-srv/inatl/longterm/fogofwar/fogofwar.htm (last accessed on May 13, 2004).

Frontline: The Gulf War. Available at http://www.pbs.org/wgbh/pages/frontline/gulf (last accessed on May 13, 2004).

Gulf Hello. Available at http://www.persiangulf.com (last accessed on May 13, 2004).

Gulf War.com. Available at http://www.gulfwar.com (last accessed on May 13, 2004).

Gulf War Index. Available at http://www.britains-smallwars.com/gulf/index.html (last accessed on May 7, 2003).

"The New Iraq." PBS *Online NewsHour.* Available at http://www.pbs.org/newshour/bb/middle_east/iraq/index.html (last accessed on May 13, 2004).

"War in Iraq." *CNN.com.* Available at http://www.cnn.com/SPECIALS/2003/iraq/index.html (last accessed on May 13, 2004).

Index

Illustrations are marked by (ill.)

I

J

K

L